the WINE LOVER'S kitchen

the WINE LOVER'S LOVER'S kitchen

DELICIOUS RECIPES FOR COOKING WITH WINE

FIONA BECKETT

photography by Mowie Kay

RYLAND PETERS & SMALL
LONDON • NEW YORK

For Will, with love. Here's a way to use all that wine…

Senior Designer Sonya Nathoo
Editors Miriam Catley
Head of Production Patricia Harrington
Creative Director Leslie Harrington
Editorial Director Julia Charles

Food stylists Rosie Reynolds,
  Sian Henley and Emily Kydd
Prop stylist Jennifer Kay
Indexer Vanessa Bird

First published in 2017 as *Wine Lover's Kitchen*. This edition published in 2024 by Ryland Peters & Small
20–21 Jockey's Fields
London WC1R 4BW
and
341 E 116th St
New York NY 10029

www.rylandpeters.com

10 9 8 7 6 5 4 3 2 1

Text copyright © Fiona Beckett 2017, 2024. Design and photographs copyright © Ryland Peters & Small 2017, 2024.

ISBN: 978-1-78879-650-7

Printed in China

A CIP record for this book is available from the British Library. US Library of Congress Cataloging-in-Publication Data has been applied for.

Notes

• Both British (Metric) and American (Imperial plus US cups) ingredients measurements are included in these recipes for your convenience, however it is important to work with one set of measurements and not alternate between the two within a recipe.
• All spoon measurements are level unless otherwise specified. 1 tablespoon is 15 ml, 1 teaspoon is 5 ml
• All eggs are medium (UK) or large (US), unless specified as large, in which case US extra-large should be used. Uncooked or partially cooked eggs should not be served to the very old, frail, young children, pregnant women or those with compromised immune systems.
• When a recipe calls for the grated zest of citrus fruit, buy unwaxed fruit and wash well before using. If you can only find treated fruit, scrub well in warm soapy water before using.
• To sterilize glass storage jars, wash them in hot, soapy water and rinse in boiling water. Place in a large saucepan and cover with hot water. With the saucepan lid on, bring the water to a boil and continue boiling for 15 minutes. Turn off the heat and leave the jars in the hot water until just before they are to be filled. Invert the jars onto a clean kitchen cloth to dry. Sterilize the lids for 5 minutes, by boiling or according to the manufacturer's instructions. Jars should be filled and sealed while they are still hot.

Contents

Wine – the magic ingredient

As a wine writer, I always seem to have a couple of opened bottles in the kitchen. Wine is as natural an addition to my cooking as olive oil. I add a quick splash to the pan to make an instant sauce for steak, pour a glass into the pan when I cook a roast, use the best part of a bottle to cook a slow, flavoursome braise, or sweeten it to make a fabulous fruit dessert. There are so many different ways to use it.

Wine adds flavour, first of all. It makes an everyday dish special, whether it's a simple tomato sauce or a stew. It adds a beautifully balanced acidity to a cream sauce or, when reduced to a few intense spoonfuls, a marvellous sauce of its own. It adds depth, body and richness to a stew, an appetizing sharpness to a pasta sauce.

Certain dishes are defined by wine – Coq au Vin, obviously, Moules Marinières, Spaghetti Vongole, a Slow-cooked Ragu just wouldn't be the same without it. You couldn't make them any other way, but you can experiment with the wine you use to get different effects. Vermentino for example would be a classic wine to use for a Spaghetti Vongole (see page 39)

but there's no reason why you couldn't use a Picpoul or an Albariño. You might not think of pouring red wine into a risotto but with the Beetroot Risotto on page 43 it works beautifully.

Can you add wine to a korma? You certainly can and although it's entirely non-traditional, it tastes the better for it. And if you've never cooked spaghetti in red wine (see page 28) – yes, really! – you haven't lived.

So don't be afraid of using wine in your cooking. Experiment just as you would with other ingredients in your store cupboard. It's one of the easiest and most effective ways to give your food that extra lift and really wow your family and friends!

10 things you need to know about cooking with wine

*Like any other ingredient you need to understand how wine works
in a dish and the best techniques for using it. Here are 10 things to remember:*

1. The wine you use needs to be drinkable. By that I mean it must be clean and fresh and, obviously, not corked. It shouldn't taste like vinegar or be so old it's lost all its fruit. If you have leftover wine decant it into a smaller bottle or container so that the air doesn't get to it. Wine that's been left open for 4–5 days is probably OK. Wine that's been sitting in your cupboard for 4–5 months generally isn't.

2. That doesn't mean it has to be the wine you normally drink. I've had great success using sweeter wines such as white Grenache or blush Zinfandel which are not particularly to my taste but which are great in a recipe or cocktail (see Frosé on page 151).

3. Don't use wines labelled as cooking wines which tend to be particularly poor quality and not that much of a saving over a cheap bottle of wine.

4. On the other hand don't feel you have to use an expensive wine. The only circumstances in which I'd advocate it is if a dish needs only a small amount of wine and you'd otherwise have to open another bottle. To steal a glass from the bottle you're planning to drink may be the cheapest way to make the dish.

5. You need a less good wine if you're cooking a slow-cooked dish like a stew than if you're quickly deglazing a pan. A good trick is to add a small dash of better wine at the end of a long braise which makes it taste as if that's the wine you've cooked with.

6. The most versatile wines are crisp, dry, unoaked whites such as Pinot Grigio and medium-bodied but not overly tannic reds like Merlot. Wines with a pronounced aromatic character such as Riesling or Gewürztraminer are less flexible, but may turn out to be delicious with, for example, a creamy sauce. Feel free to experiment.

7. Fortified wines such as Sherry, Madeira and Marsala are great for cooking. A small quantity adds strength, depth and often a welcome sweetness.

8. Reducing a wine by simmering will accentuate its dominant character such as sweetness, tannin or acidity. But it's a useful way of concentrating flavour when you want to add a small amount to a dish or dressing.

9. A wine-based marinade will tenderize meat but it will change the flavour and make it more 'gamey' if you do it for longer than a couple of hours. You should also discard the marinade unless you're going to cook it well. (See the Red Wine Marinated Venison Steaks on page 98.)

10. Even in recipes that feature a significant amount of wine you usually need another ingredient such as stock, cream or passata/strained tomatoes to balance it. A homemade chicken or vegetable stock is a boon. Freeze leftover wine in an ice cube tray and keep the cubes handy in a freezer bag to add to a dish.

Finally, a question I'm often asked. If you cook with wine is there any alcohol left in the dish? There is a widespread misconception that it all cooks out but unless you're cooking the dish for 3 hours or more there will be a residue depending on how much wine you've used. Worth bearing in mind if you're cooking for kids or non-drinkers.

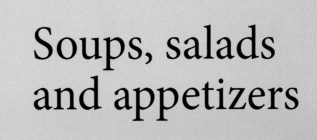

Soups, salads and appetizers

Red chicory, roquefort and hazelnut salad with moscatel dressing

It might not occur to you to use wine in a salad dressing but in fact it saves you from having to buy a lot of expensive flavoured wine vinegar. For this recipe you want a light Moscatel not a dark sticky one.

50 g/^{1}/$_3$ cup roasted, skinned hazelnuts*
2 heads of red or green chicory
2 Comice or Conference pears, peeled and cut into 8 segments
100 g/^{3}/$_4$ cup Roquefort, roughly crumbled

FOR THE DRESSING
2 tablespoons light sweet Moscatel or southern French Muscat, such as Muscat de St Jean de Minervois
1 tablespoon white wine vinegar
2 tablespoons mild olive oil
sea salt and freshly ground white pepper

Serves 4

Preheat the oven to 180°C (350°F) Gas 4.

Freshen up the hazelnuts by roasting them in the oven or toasting them in a dry frying pan/skillet. Set aside to cool and chop roughly.

Separate out the chicory leaves and place in a bowl of iced water for 15–20 minutes. Drain and pat the leaves dry with a kitchen towel.

Make the dressing. Measure out the sweet wine, white wine vinegar and the olive oil into a jam jar and give it a good shake. Alternatively put the ingredients in a bowl and whisk together. Adjust the amount of wine, vinegar or oil to taste – add a dash more wine if it needs the sweetness or vinegar if it needs the acidity. Season with sea salt and freshly ground white pepper, to taste.

Arrange the salad on individual plates starting with a pile of chicory leaves, then the pear segments and Roquefort. Re-whisk or shake the dressing, check the seasoning and spoon over the salad. Top with the chopped hazelnuts.

*If you can't find skinned hazelnuts roast them with their skins on until dark brown then rub off the skins with a kitchen towel.

What to drink

A lush white wine such as an oak-aged Sauvignon or Sauvignon-Semillon blend.

Smoked duck, mandarin and pecan salad with pinot noir and pomegranate dressing

Red wine can be used in place of wine vinegar to make a deliciously fruity dressing. Making a red wine reduction like this is a thrifty way to use up leftover wine, and it will keep in the refrigerator for several days.

3 mandarin oranges
  or other small sweet
  oranges
100 g/3^1/2 oz. lamb's
  lettuce/mâche
  or watercress
225 g/8 oz. smoked duck
  breast, sliced
100 g/3/4 cup candied
  pecans* or walnuts

FOR THE DRESSING
225 ml/scant 1 cup
  Chilean or other
  inexpensive Pinot Noir,
  or another fruity red
  wine
1^1/2 tablespoons light
  muscovado sugar
100 ml/^{1}/3 cup plus
  1 tablespoon light
  olive oil
1 medium pomegranate
^{1}/2–1 teaspoon
  pomegranate molasses
  or balsamic vinegar
sea salt and freshly
  ground black pepper

Serves 6

Peel and slice the oranges horizontally, reserving any juice. Cut the larger slices in half to make half-moon shapes.

To make the dressing, put the wine in a small saucepan, bring to the boil, then lower the heat. Simmer for 10–15 minutes or until the wine has reduced by two-thirds (leaving about 5 tablespoons). Remove the pan from the heat, stir in the muscovado sugar and let cool.

Once cool, whisk in the olive oil and season to taste with salt and pepper. Cut the pomegranate in half and scoop the seeds into a bowl, catching any juice. Discard the pith and tip the seeds and juice, along with any juice from the oranges, into the dressing. Add the pomegranate molasses or balsamic vinegar to taste. Stir well.

Divide the lamb's lettuce/mâche or watercress between six plates and arrange the duck breast and orange slices on top. Scatter over the candied pecans or walnuts. Give the dressing a quick whisk, then spoon it over the salad. Serve immediately.

* If you can't find candied pecans, put 100 g/3/4 cup pecans in a dry, non-stick frying pan/skillet and sprinkle over 1 teaspoon caster/granulated sugar. Toast gently over medium heat for a couple of minutes, shaking the pan frequently, until the nuts are crisp and the sugar has caramelized.

What to drink

The dressing is quite intense, so choose an equally powerful New World Pinot Noir from, for example, California, Oregon, Chile or Central Otago in New Zealand to stand up to it.

White onion and bay leaf soup with raclette and toasted hazelnuts

I tasted this soup at one of my favourite Bristol restaurants, Wallfish, and begged the chef, Seldon Curry, for the recipe. It sounds like a lot of onions and butter – it is – but trust me it works. He used a local Somerset cheese called Ogleshield but I'm suggesting the more widely available Raclette here.

125 g/1^1/8 sticks butter
1.25 kg/44 oz. white onions, finely sliced
1 teaspoon salt
2 bay leaves
3 tablespoons dry white wine
25 g/3 tablespoons plain/all-purpose flour
600 ml/2^1/2 cups whole/full-fat milk, plus extra if you need it
175 g/2 cups plus 1 teaspoon grated Raclette or Ogleshield cheese

FOR THE GARNISH
3 tablespoons rapeseed oil
75 g/^{1}/2 cup roasted hazelnuts, roughly chopped
2 tablespoons freshly chopped parsley

Serves 4–6

Melt the butter in a large pan and tip in the onions. Stir thoroughly then add the salt, bay leaves and wine. Put a lid on the pan and cook over a low heat for about 45 minutes until deliciously soft and sweet.

Sprinkle over the flour, stir and cook for 5 minutes then gradually add the milk, stirring until smooth, and continue to cook over a low heat for about 15 minutes. Remove the bay leaves, add the Raclette then take off the heat, cool and pass in batches through a blender until smooth*. You can sieve/strain it for extra smoothness if you want. Return to the pan, check the seasoning, adding a touch more milk if you need to thin it down.

To serve, ladle into warm bowls, drizzle the rapeseed oil over the soup and sprinkle over the chopped hazelnuts and parsley.

* If you only have a food processor rather than a blender I'd suggest straining the onions after you have cooked them then processing them into a purée, adding about half the reserved liquid. Sprinkle the flour into the remainder of the liquid then cook it out and add the milk as described above. Add this mixture back to the purée along with the cheese and whizz again.

What to drink

A smooth, dry white wine such as a Soave or Roero Arneis.

Summer pea and asparagus velouté

A velouté is a silky-smooth soup made with good stock and cream and a perfect vehicle for the new season's peas and asparagus. A splash of white wine makes it even more luxurious. You could make it with frozen peas but it wouldn't taste as good as they're grown for sweetness these days. Similarly it tastes much better if you use homemade stock and I'm afraid chicken is better than veggie stock in this recipe.

250-g/9-oz. bunch
of asparagus
30 g/¼ stick butter
1 small onion, finely chopped
2 tablespoons smooth dry
white wine, such as white
Burgundy or other subtly
oaked Chardonnay
600 ml/2½ cups light chicken
stock, preferably homemade
200 g/1⅓ cups fresh peas,
podded
double/heavy cream, to serve
sea salt and freshly ground
white pepper

Makes 4 small bowls

Rinse the asparagus. Break off the tough woody ends about one-third of the way up each spear and discard. Slice off the tips about half way down what remains of the spear and set aside. Finely slice the middle section of the spears and cut the tips in half or quarters depending on how thick they are. Set the tips aside.

Heat the butter in a lidded pan and tip in the onion and sliced asparagus. Season with salt, put a lid on the pan and cook over a low to medium heat for about 5 minutes until the vegetables are tender.

Add 300 ml/1¼ cups of the stock to the pan and bring to the boil. Add the peas and cover and simmer for about 3–4 minutes until tender. You want to cook them for the shortest possible time to preserve their colour.

Strain the vegetables, keeping the cooking liquid. Put the vegetables in a blender and whizz until smooth, adding back the liquid you cooked them in and the remaining stock. Pass the soup through a sieve/strainer back into the pan. Cook the asparagus tips briefly in a steamer or microwave. Quickly heat through the soup.

Divide the asparagus spears between four warm bowls and ladle the soup on top. Add a swirl of cream to each bowl and serve immediately.

What to drink

A crisp dry white wine such as a Chablis or other white Burgundy. Other crisp dry whites such as Albariño or Greco di Tufo would also work well.

Warm scallop salad with crispy pancetta and parsnip chips

Cooking scallops is a bit like cooking a steak. You can sear them, then make a delicious dressing with a dash of wine mingled with the pan juices.

12 medium-sized fresh
   scallops, removed from
   their shells
1 tablespoon olive oil, plus
   extra for dressing the salad
100 g/3½ oz. pancetta cubes
4 tablespoons Chardonnay,
   Viognier or other full-bodied
   white wine
2 tablespoons fish stock
   or water
1 tablespoon double/heavy
   cream or crème fraîche
about 80 g/3 oz. mixed salad
   leaves
sea salt and freshly ground
   black pepper

FOR THE PARSNIP CRISPS
1 medium parsnip, peeled
vegetable oil, for
   deep-frying
sea salt

Serves 4

To make the parsnip crisps, cut off the root end of the parsnip to leave a piece about 10 cm/4 in. long and 3–4 cm/1¼–1½ in. wide at its narrowest point. Using a mandoline or a vegetable peeler, shave off very thin slices.

Fill one-quarter of a wok with vegetable oil. Heat the oil until very hot, about 190°C (375°F), or until a cube of bread turns golden in 40 seconds. Add the parsnip slices and fry in batches for about 30–60 seconds until brown and crisp. Remove the crisps with a slotted spoon, drain on paper towels and sprinkle lightly with salt.

Season the scallops on both sides with salt and pepper. Heat 1 tablespoon olive oil in a frying pan/skillet, add the pancetta cubes and fry for about 3–4 minutes, turning occasionally, until crisp. Remove from the pan with a slotted spoon, drain on paper towels, then set aside and keep warm.

Pour off the fat from the frying pan/skillet, then return the pan to the heat for about 1 minute until almost smoking. Add the scallops to the pan and cook for 2–3 minutes, depending on their thickness, turning them over halfway through. Remove them from the pan, set aside and keep them warm.

Pour the white wine into the pan and let it bubble up. Continue cooking until the wine has reduced by half. Add the fish stock or water and keep the liquid bubbling until it has reduced to just over a couple of tablespoons. Pour any juices that have accumulated under the scallops into the pan, stir in the cream or crème fraîche and season to taste with salt and pepper. Warm through for a few seconds, then remove the pan from the heat.

Divide the salad leaves between four plates, drizzle with a little olive oil and season lightly. Scatter over the pancetta cubes and the parsnip crisps. Put three scallops on each plate, spoon over the pan juices and serve immediately.

What to drink

A white Burgundy or other cool-climate Chardonnay would be delicious with this dish.

Mushroom, mustard and madeira soup

A rich, intensely delicious soup that makes a good first course for a dinner party.

75 g/³/₄ stick butter, plus a little extra for frying the mushrooms

1 medium onion, finely chopped

1 large garlic clove, finely chopped

500 g/18 oz. chestnut mushrooms

2 tablespoons Madeira or Oloroso sherry

1 teaspoon dried porcini powder (optional)*

1 litre/4 cups mushroom or vegetable stock*

1 medium potato, peeled and sliced

2 teaspoons wholegrain mustard

sea salt and freshly ground black pepper

lemon juice, to taste

double/heavy cream, to serve

Serves 4–6

Heat the butter in a large saucepan or casserole and add the chopped onion and garlic. Cook over a low heat until soft.

Wipe the mushrooms clean, trim the stalks and thinly slice, reserving a good few slices for the garnish. Tip the remaining mushrooms into the butter, stir and cook for about 15 minutes until the mushrooms are brown and the liquid has all but evaporated. Stir in the Madeira or sherry and the porcini powder if using.

Add the stock, bring to the boil then add the sliced potato. Simmer until the potato is soft. Strain, reserving the liquid and blitz in a blender or food processor, gradually adding back the reserved liquid until you have a smooth soup. Return to the pan, add the mustard and reheat gently without boiling. Check the seasoning, adding salt, pepper and lemon juice to taste.

To serve, fry the reserved mushroom slices briefly in a little butter. Ladle the soup into warm bowls, top with a swirl of cream and scatter the mushroom slices over the top.

* If you use vegetable stock I'd add some dried porcini powder to the mushrooms to intensify the flavour.

What to drink

A glass of Amontillado sherry is perfect with this or you could drink a rich Chardonnay.

Luxurious cheese fondue

If you're making a dish as simple as fondue you need to use top quality cheese. Emmental and Gruyère are traditional but once you've got the hang of it you can play around with other alternatives.

425 g/7 cups finely sliced or coarsely grated cheese, with rinds removed, such as:
(150 g/1¹/₃ cups Gruyère or Comté, 150 g/ 1¹/₃ cups Beaufort and 125 g/1 cup Emmental, or 225 g/2 cups Gruyère and 200 g/ 1²/₃ cups Emmental)
2 teaspoons potato flour or corn flour/ cornstarch
1 garlic clove, halved

175 ml/³/₄ cup Muscadet, or other very dry white wine
1 tablespoon kirsch (optional)
freshly ground nutmeg and black pepper
sourdough, pain de campagne or ciabatta, to serve

A cast iron fondue pan and burner

Serves 2

Toss the sliced or grated cheese with the flour. Set aside until it comes to room temperature.

Rub the inside of the pan with the cut garlic. Start off the fondue on your cooker. Pour in the wine and heat until almost boiling. Remove from the heat and tip in about one-third of the cheese. Keep breaking up the cheese with a wooden spoon using a zig-zag motion as if you were using a wire whisk. (Stirring it round and round as you do with a sauce makes it more likely that the cheese will separate from the liquid.)

Once the cheese has begun to melt return it over a very low heat, stirring continuously. Gradually add the remaining cheese until you have a smooth, thick mass (this takes about 10 minutes, less with practice). If it seems too thick add some more hot wine. Add the kirsch, if you like, and season with nutmeg and pepper.

Place over your fondue burner and serve with bite-size chunks of sourdough or country bread.

Use long fondue forks to dip the bread in, stirring the fondue to prevent it solidifying.

What to drink

A Swiss white such as Chasselas if you can get hold of it or a white wine from the Savoie region of France such as Roussette would be traditional. Otherwise any crisp, dry white, such as Muscadet, will do.

Pasta and grains

Red wine spaghetti with olives and anchovies

I stumbled across a recipe for cooking spaghetti in red wine when I was researching this book. It sounded so bizarre I had to give it a try and can vouch for the fact that it's delicious! It would be a bit expensive to make for a crowd so this quantity will feed 2–3. And my version is dairy-free.

500 ml/2 cups plus 2 tablespoons full-bodied fruity red wine

250 g/9 oz. wholewheat spaghetti

50-g/2-oz. can of anchovies

1–2 tablespoons olive oil

3 garlic cloves, finely sliced

70 g/2/3 cup pitted olives with herbs

1/2 teaspoon Turkish dried chilli flakes/red pepper flakes

3 tablespoons passata or 1 tablespoon concentrated tomato purée/paste

25 g/1 cup freshly chopped flat leaf parsley

sea salt

Serves 2–3

Measure 400 ml/1¾ cups of the red wine into a saucepan and add 500 ml/2 cups plus 2 tablespoons water. Bring to the boil, add a teaspoon of salt and partially cook the spaghetti for about 7–8 minutes. Drain, reserving half a cup of the cooking liquid. Meanwhile drain the can of anchovies, reserving the oil. Add the oil from the anchovies plus enough additional olive oil to make 3 tablespoons in total into a frying pan/skillet and fry the garlic slices over a very low heat.

Chop the anchovies and halve the olives. Add the chilli/red pepper flakes to the garlic, stir in the passata or tomato purée/paste and tip in the reserved pasta cooking water and the rest of the wine. Bring to the boil, add the anchovies and olives and simmer for a few minutes. Tip the partially cooked spaghetti into the sauce and leave over a low to medium heat until most of the liquid is absorbed. Add about three-quarters of the chopped parsley to the pasta and toss well. Serve in warm bowls with the remaining parsley sprinkled on top.

What to drink

The same wine you use to make the dish or a hearty Sicilian red like a Nero d'Avola.

Slow-cooked ragu

I wouldn't presume to claim this was an authentic Bolognese as everyone's Bolognese is different. The key is the long, slow cooking, which transports this family favourite into a luxury pasta dish. It may seem a lot of liquid to begin with but the cooking time will cause much of that liquid to evaporate.

2 tablespoons olive oil

40 g/3 tablespoons butter

1 medium onion, finely chopped

1 medium carrot, finely chopped

1 celery stalk/stick, finely chopped

1 garlic clove, finely chopped

50 g/2 oz. Parma ham/ prosciutto or other air-dried ham

400 g/14 oz. lean minced/ground meat (a combination of beef or veal and pork works best)

175 ml/3/4 cup white wine

300 g/10½ oz. good quality artisanal passata/strained tomatoes

200 ml/1 scant cup chicken stock (preferably homemade)

1 bay leaf

3 tablespoons double/ heavy cream

sea salt and freshly ground black pepper

buttered tagliatelle or fettuccine, to serve

freshly grated Parmesan, to serve

Serves 4

In a large heavy-based pan, heat the oil and add the butter. Add the finely chopped onion, carrot and celery, give it a good stir, put a lid on the pan and cook over a low heat for about 10 minutes until soft. Add the garlic and cook for another couple of minutes. Add the Parma ham/prosciutto and minced/ground meat in two batches, turning it with a spoon until it is slightly coloured. Pour in the white wine and simmer until reduced by about one-third. Add the passata/strained tomato, chicken stock and bay leaf. Season with salt and black pepper and leave uncovered on a very low heat to cook for about 2–2½ hours, stirring occasionally.

After this time the sauce should be creamy but shouldn't be too thick – add a bit of extra stock if it needs thinning down. Check the seasoning and stir in the cream. Serve with buttered tagliatelle or fettuccine and freshly grated Parmesan.

What to drink

You could drink the same white wine you've used to make this dish but I actually prefer a light red like a Rosso di Montalcino.

Sticky pork mac 'n' cheese

Fortified wines such as port and sherry can be used to quickly caramelize meat like the belly pork in this wickedly sinful version of macaroni cheese.

1 tablespoon plus 1 teaspoon olive or sunflower oil

600 g/21 oz. pork belly rashers, preferably organic, cut into small cubes

1 large or 2 medium onions, thinly sliced

50 g/3½ tablespoons butter

40 g/heaping ¼ cup plain/all-purpose flour

600 ml/2½ cups whole/full-fat milk

1 bay leaf

a pinch of freshly ground nutmeg

250 g/2 cups macaroni or penne pasta

125 g/1⅓ cups mature Gouda or Cheddar, grated

75 ml/⅓ cup 10-year-old Tawny Port or Marsala

75 ml/⅓ cup chicken stock

30 g/⅓ cup grated Parmesan mixed with 30 g/⅓ cup fresh breadcrumbs

sea salt and freshly ground black pepper

Serves 4

Preheat the oven to 190°C (375°F) Gas 5.

Heat the oil in an ovenproof frying pan/skillet over a medium heat and fry the pork pieces. Once the fat starts to run stir in the sliced onion, cook for a minute or two, season then transfer to the preheated oven and cook uncovered for about 30 minutes, stirring from time to time until the pork is crisp and the onion caramelized.

Heat 40 g/3 tablespoons of the butter in a non-stick saucepan, stir in the flour then take the pan off the heat and gradually add the milk, stirring constantly. Put the pan back on the hob, increase the heat then bring the sauce gradually up to simmering point. Add the bay leaf, season then leave on a very low heat for the sauce to thicken.

Bring a large pan of water to the boil, add salt and cook the pasta for the time recommended on the packet. Drain, reserving a little of the cooking water and stir in a teaspoon of olive oil.

Once the pork is cooked pour in the port, let it bubble up and reduce then add the chicken stock and deglaze the pan. Season with salt.

Remove the bay leaf from the white sauce, stir in the cheese and adjust the seasoning, adding a little of the reserved pasta cooking water to thin the sauce if needed.

Preheat the grill/broiler. Tip the pasta into the sauce, mix thoroughly then loosely stir in the pork and juices. Tip into a shallow ovenproof dish and top with the breadcrumbs and cheese. Place under but not too close to the heat, and grill/broil until the top is brown and bubbling. Leave for 5 minutes before serving.

What to drink

I like a rich Chardonnay with mac 'n' cheese but you could serve a ripe red like a Merlot.

Rigatoni with aubergine/eggplant, sausage and zinfandel sauce

This is a really robust pasta dish that's perfect to serve in cold weather. The wine gives a richer, more warming flavour than the usual tomato-based sauce.

350 g/³/₄ lb. Italian sausages or other coarsely ground 100 per cent pork sausages

4 tablespoons olive oil

1 medium aubergine/eggplant, cut into cubes

1 medium onion, finely chopped

1 red (bell) pepper, deseeded and cut into 2-cm/³/₄-in. cubes

1 rounded tablespoon tomato purée/paste

2 garlic cloves, crushed

1 teaspoon dried oregano

175 ml/³/₄ cup Zinfandel or other full-bodied, fruity red wine

175 ml/³/₄ cup fresh chicken stock, or light vegetable stock made from 1 teaspoon vegetable bouillon powder

350 g/3³/₄ cups dried pasta tubes, such as rigatoni or penne

4 tablespoons freshly chopped parsley

sea salt and freshly ground black pepper

Serves 4

Slit the sausage skins with a sharp knife, peel them off and discard. Roughly chop the sausage meat. Heat 1 tablespoon olive oil in a large frying pan/skillet or wok, add the sausage meat, breaking it up with a spatula or wooden spoon, and fry until lightly golden. Using a slotted spoon, remove the meat from the pan and set aside.

Add 2 more tablespoons of the oil to the pan, add the aubergine/eggplant and fry for 3–4 minutes until it starts to brown. Add the remaining oil and the chopped onion and fry for 1–2 minutes. Add the red (bell) pepper and fry for 1–2 minutes more. Return the sausagemeat to the pan, stir in the tomato purée/paste and cook for 1 minute. Add the garlic, oregano and wine and simmer until the wine has reduced by half. Stir in the stock and let simmer over a low heat for about 10 minutes.

Meanwhile, cook the pasta. Bring a large saucepan of lightly salted water to the boil. Add the pasta and cook for about 10 minutes until al dente, or according to the instructions on the packet. When the pasta is just cooked, spoon off a couple of tablespoons of the cooking water and stir it into the wine sauce. Drain the pasta thoroughly, then tip it into the sauce. Add 3 tablespoons of the parsley and mix well. Remove the pan from the heat, cover and let stand for 2–3 minutes for the flavours to amalgamate.

Check the seasoning, adding salt and pepper to taste, then spoon the pasta and sauce into four warm serving bowls. Serve immediately, sprinkled with the remaining parsley.

What to drink

A Zinfandel would be the obvious choice, but any robust medium- to full-bodied red would work well.

Roast squash, corn and quinoa salad with dukkah

A lovely late summer salad that not only includes Chardonnay but also goes brilliantly well with it too. I like to serve it just warm or at room temperature but you can make it ahead if you wish. You could also use other in-season vegetables such as red (bell) peppers or fennel.

4 tablespoons olive or rapeseed oil

1 small or half a larger butternut squash, deseeded, peeled and cut into small cubes

1 head of corn, cut into 4 chunks

150 g/5¹/₂ oz. carrots, thickly sliced

¹/₂ teaspoon ras el hanout or another Moroccan spice blend

150 g/1 cup quinoa

75 ml/¹/₃ cup Chardonnay

1 tablespoon Chardonnay vinegar or other white wine vinegar

2 heaped tablespoons freshly chopped flat leaf parsley or coriander/cilantro

3 tablespoons dukkah* or sesame seeds

¹/₂ bunch of salad onions, trimmed, and cut lengthwise into thin strips

sea salt and freshly ground black pepper

Serves 4

Preheat the oven to 200°C (400°F) Gas 6.

Measure 3 tablespoons of the oil into a roasting pan and add the prepared squash, corn and carrots. Turn the vegetables in the oil and season with salt, pepper and the ras el hanout. Roast for about 30–35 minutes in the preheated oven until the vegetables are cooked but still retain some bite. Set aside on a plate. Deglaze the roasting pan with the Chardonnay.

Meanwhile cook the quinoa following the instructions on the packet. Drain if necessary and spread out in a shallow dish.

Cut the corn off the cob and tip it and the other vegetables into the quinoa along with the pan juices. Add the vinegar and a little extra oil if necessary and stir in the parsley or coriander/cilantro and 2 tablespoons of the dukkah. Heat the remaining oil and fry the onion strips briefly until lightly browned. Scatter over the surface of the salad and sprinkle over the remaining dukkah.

* Dukkah is an Egyptian blend of roasted seeds and spices that makes a delicious dip or salad topping.

What to drink

The same Chardonnay you've used to make the salad. A rich Viognier or Chenin Blanc would also be delicious.

Spaghetti vongole with vermentino

This is one of the quickest and most delicious pasta dishes ever which simply relies on great ingredients – fresh clams, Italian pasta and good wine. I suggest Vermentino because I love it and it works particularly well but you can use almost any crisp, fresh unoaked Italian wine. Coriander/cilantro isn't traditional, of course, but I like it with the chilli/chile.

250 g/9 oz. small fresh clams

100–125 g/3^{1}/$_{2}$–4^{1}/$_{2}$ oz. good-quality Italian spaghetti or linguine

2 tablespoons olive oil

1 large garlic clove, finely chopped

^{1}/$_{2}$ small red chilli/chile, deseeded and finely chopped or ^{1}/$_{4}$ teaspoon chilli/hot red pepper flakes

50 ml/3^{1}/$_{2}$ tablespoons Vermentino or other dry white Italian wine

2 tablespoons freshly chopped coriander/cilantro or flat leaf parsley

a good squeeze of lemon juice

sea salt

Serves 1 (sometimes it's good to treat yourself)

Tip the clams into a bowl of cold water, give them a good swirl and leave them for half an hour to get rid of any grit. Measure out and prepare your other ingredients. When you're ready to cook bring 1.5 litres/6 cups plus 4 tablespoons water to the boil, salt generously, add the spaghetti and cook according to the instructions on the packet.

While the spaghetti is cooking heat the oil over a low heat in another saucepan and cook the garlic and chilli/chile for a minute or two. Turn up the heat, add the clams and then the wine. Cover the pan and cook, shaking the pan occasionally for 2–3 minutes. All the clams should be open – discard any that aren't and take the pan off the heat.

When the spaghetti is cooked, spoon off about 3 tablespoons of the cooking water and drain. Tip the clams, chilli/chile and garlic into the spaghetti, along with the reserved water and chopped coriander/cilantro or parsley and toss well. Check the seasoning – I like to add a squeeze of lemon juice and serve in a warm bowl.

What to drink

The same wine you use to make the dish – yet another reason for using something decent!

Wild mushroom and champagne risotto

It may seem wantonly extravagant to use Champagne in your cooking, but you need only a glass and the bonus is that you can drink the rest with the risotto. I suggest using a Blanc de Noirs – it has just the right toasty richness for this recipe.

250 g/9 oz. wild mushrooms or 225 g/8 oz. chestnut mushrooms and 25 g/3/4 oz. dried porcini, soaked for 15 minutes in warm water

2 tablespoons light olive oil

80 g/3/4 stick unsalted butter

1.2 litres/5 cups light chicken or vegetable stock

1 medium onion, finely chopped

300 g/1 1/2 cups risotto rice, such as arborio or carnaroli

125 ml/1/2 cup Champagne or other dry sparkling white wine

3 heaped tablespoons freshly grated Parmesan cheese, plus extra to serve

sea salt and freshly ground black pepper

Serves 6

Clean the fresh mushrooms by lightly brushing or wiping them with a damp cloth, then slice them thinly. Drain the porcini, if using, and slice them. Reserve the soaking water.

Heat a medium frying pan/skillet. Add half the olive oil and half the butter to the pan and fry the mushrooms for about 4 minutes until lightly browned. Remove the pan from the heat, cover and set aside. Heat the stock in a saucepan until almost boiling, then reduce the heat and simmer.

Meanwhile, heat the remaining oil and half the remaining butter in a large, heavy-based saucepan. Add the onion and cook over a low heat for 4–5 minutes until soft. Increase the heat slightly, add the rice to the pan and stir until well coated with the butter and the grains turn opaque, about 3 minutes.

Add the Champagne or other sparkling wine to the pan – it will sizzle and evaporate almost immediately. Add the sliced porcini, if using, then begin adding the hot stock, a large ladleful at a time, stirring gently until the liquid has been almost absorbed by the rice. Add the next ladleful of stock and repeat until the rice is tender and creamy but still has some 'bite' to it. This should take 15–20 minutes.

About 5 minutes before the end of the cooking time, stir in most of the fresh mushrooms, reserving a few for serving. When the risotto is ready, stir in the remaining butter and the Parmesan and season to taste with salt and pepper. If you've used dried porcini, add 1–2 tablespoons of the strained soaking water for extra flavour. Cover the pan and leave to stand for a few minutes while you reheat the reserved mushrooms. Serve the risotto in warmed bowls with the sautéed mushrooms sprinkled on top and a little extra grated Parmesan.

What to drink

Blanc de Noirs Champagne or whatever you used in the risotto.

Beetroot and pinot risotto

The sweetness of Pinot chimes in beautifully with the earthy flavour of the beetroot/beets in this vegetarian risotto. Use the freshest possible beetroot/beets you can find for the deepest colour and flavour. (It's worth wearing a pair of disposable plastic gloves when you cut them up so you don't stain your hands.)

3 tablespoons olive oil
200 g/7 oz. red onion, roughly chopped
3–4 fresh beetroot/beets, ideally with their leaves
1 garlic clove, crushed
225 g/1¹/8 cups arborio or other risotto rice
150 ml/²/3 cup inexpensive fruity Pinot Noir e.g., from Chile

1 litre/4 cups hot miso stock made with miso bouillon powder
100 g/3¹/2 oz. mild, crumbly goat's cheese
a few sprigs of fresh dill or a handful of chives, chopped

Serves 4

Heat the oil in a large frying pan/skillet and fry the onion over a moderate heat for 5 minutes. Peel the beetroot/beets (reserving the leaves) and cut into small cubes, add to the pan, season with salt and pepper and cook for another 10 minutes.

Add the crushed garlic, cook for a minute then tip in the rice and cook, stirring, for 2–3 minutes. Pour in the Pinot Noir and let it evaporate. Add the hot stock, about 50 ml/3¹/2 tablespoons at a time, stirring occasionally and letting each addition be absorbed before adding the next.

Once the rice is cooked (about 20 minutes), add a little extra stock or water, check the seasoning and leave for 5 minutes. Warm your serving bowls. Wash the beetroot/beet leaves if you have some, strip from the stalks and cook down in a saucepan without any extra water. Place a few leaves in each bowl, spoon in the risotto, top with crumbled goat's cheese and sprinkle with chopped dill or chives.

What to drink

The Pinot Noir you used in the recipe.

Fish and seafood

Moules marinières with muscadet

This classic bistro dish is a wonderful way to enjoy mussels. The French would generally use a basic white vin de table, but I think it tastes particularly good with Muscadet.

1 kg/2¼ lb. fresh mussels

3 tablespoons light olive oil or sunflower oil

1 medium onion, finely chopped

2 garlic cloves, finely chopped

100 ml/⅓ cup plus 1 tablespoon Muscadet or other crisp dry white wine

3 heaped tablespoons freshly chopped parsley

your choice of chips/fries, mayonnaise and crusty bread, to serve

Serves 2

Tip the mussels into a sink full of cold water and give them a good swirl. Drain off the water, fill up the sink again and swirl the mussels once more. Discard any mussels that are open. Using a small, sharp knife, remove the hairy 'beards'. Transfer the mussels to a large bowl of fresh cold water.

Heat the oil in a large saucepan or deep flameproof casserole, add the onion and cook over a low heat for 5–6 minutes until beginning to soften. Stir in the garlic, pour in the wine, then increase the heat and bring to the boil. Drain the mussels and tip them into the pan. Turn them over in the sauce, cover the pan and cook over a high heat for 3 minutes, shaking the pan occasionally. Remove the lid and check the mussels are open. If not, cover and cook for 1 minute more. Discard any mussels that haven't opened, then sprinkle over the parsley.

Serve immediately in deep bowls accompanied by chips/fries and mayonnaise (wickedly delicious) or crusty bread.

What to drink

The remaining Muscadet would go well, or use any simple, carafe-style French white.

Cioppino

Cioppino hails from San Francisco and is a rustic stew made with fresh fish and shellfish.

FOR THE STOCK
3 tablespoons olive oil
1 medium onion, finely chopped
3 garlic cloves, crushed
1 teaspoon dried oregano
2 tablespoons dry vermouth, such as Noilly Prat (optional)
175 ml/³/₄ cup dry white wine such as Picpoul de Pinet or Pinot Grigio
400 g/14 oz. fresh tomatoes, skinned, deseeded and chopped
400 g/14 oz. can cherry tomatoes
500 ml/2 cups plus 2 tablespoons fish stock or a mixture of fish stock and clam juice
a few parsley stalks
1 bay leaf
Tabasco or other hot pepper sauce
sea salt and freshly ground black pepper

FOR THE STEW
450 g/16 oz. clams or mussels
1 tablespoon olive oil
30 g/¹/₄ stick butter
1 medium onion, sliced
2 celery stalks, trimmed and sliced
50 ml/3¹/₂ tablespoons dry white wine
600 g/21 oz. firm white fish such as cod cut into chunks
300 g/10¹/₂ oz. raw prawns/shrimp
3 tablespoons freshly chopped flat leaf parsley
sea salt and freshly ground black pepper

TO SERVE
12–16 slices day-old baguette
olive oil
2 garlic cloves, cut in half

Serves 6–8

What to drink

You can drink the same white wine you use to make the stew but a dry Provencal rosé is also particularly delicious.

To make the stock, heat the oil in a large saucepan add the onion and cook over a low heat for 5 minutes until beginning to soften. Add the garlic, stir and cook for 1 minute then stir in the oregano. Turn up the heat and add the vermouth, if using, and the wine. Bubble up until it's reduced by at least half then tip in the fresh tomatoes. Stir, put a lid on the pan and cook over a low heat, stirring occasionally, until the tomatoes have broken down. Add the cherry tomatoes and fish stock and bring to the boil. Add the parsley, bay leaf and season with salt, pepper and a few shakes of Tabasco. Simmer for 15–20 minutes and set aside, removing the parsley stalks and bay leaf.

Preheat the oven to 190°C (375°F) Gas 5.

Lay the sliced baguette out on a baking sheet. Drizzle both sides of the baguette with olive oil and bake for about 10–15 minutes until crisp. Set aside to cool. Soak the clams or mussels in cold water for at least 30 minutes, scrubbing and removing the 'beards' if necessary. Heat the olive oil in a large pan, add the butter and cook the onion and celery over a low heat for 5 minutes until soft. Pour in the wine, let it reduce then turn up the heat and add the clams or mussels. Cover the pan and cook for a couple of minutes until the shells open up. Take the pan off the heat and remove any clams or mussels that haven't opened. Heat the reserved tomato stock. Place the fish and the prawns/shrimp on top of the clams or mussels and pour over the hot stock. Bring back to the boil and simmer for a minute until the fish is cooked. Carefully fold in the parsley. Rub the toasted baguette with the cut garlic cloves. Serve the stew in warm bowls handing round the toasted baguette to float on top or break into the soup.

Thai-spiced salmon with cucumber salad

Cooking with wine has the image of being calorific, but this fresh-tasting, zingy fish dish couldn't be lighter.

4 thick salmon fillets, 150 g/5½ oz. each

300 ml/1¼ cups dry white wine, such as Pinot Grigio or Muscadet

2 garlic cloves

a small chunk of ginger, peeled and thickly sliced

1 stalk of lemongrass, cut into 3

a few fresh coriander/cilantro stalks

6 fresh or dried kaffir lime leaves

8 peppercorns

½ teaspoon sea salt

1 lime, cut into wedges, to serve

FOR THE CUCUMBER SALAD

freshly squeezed juice of 2 limes

1½ tablespoons fish sauce

1 garlic clove, crushed

2-cm/¾-in. piece of ginger, peeled and grated

1 small red chilli/chile, deseeded and very finely chopped

½–1 teaspoon caster/granulated sugar

⅓ cucumber, peeled, deseeded and thinly sliced

1 green (bell) pepper, deseeded and very thinly sliced

1 large carrot, quartered and cut into very thin strips

3 spring onions/scallions, thinly sliced

3 tablespoons freshly chopped coriander/cilantro

3 tablespoons freshly chopped mint leaves

freshly ground black pepper

Serves 4

Fit the salmon fillets snugly in a single layer in the bottom of a large saucepan. Pour over the white wine and enough cold water to cover the fish, then remove the salmon fillets and set aside. Add the garlic, ginger, lemongrass, coriander/cilantro stalks, kaffir lime leaves and peppercorns to the pan and bring to the boil. Add the salt, reduce the heat and simmer for 15 minutes.

Gently slide the salmon fillets into the poaching liquid ensuring they are completely covered with the stock, if not, add more boiling water to cover. Bring the stock back to the boil and cook for 2 minutes. Remove the pan from the heat, cover and let cool completely – at least 5 hours or overnight.

To make the cucumber salad, put the lime juice, fish sauce, garlic, ginger and chilli/chile in a bowl and mix well. Add 2–3 tablespoons water and season to taste with pepper and sugar (it shouldn't need any salt). Add the cucumber, (bell) pepper, carrot, spring onions/scallions, coriander/cilantro and mint leaves and toss well. Serve the salmon fillets accompanied by the salad and a few lime wedges for squeezing.

What to drink

I often enjoy this zingy fresh dish without wine, but a bone dry Riesling from Germany, Austria or Alsace works very well with these flavours.

Quick tiger prawns with pinot grigio, fresh tomato and basil sauce

The combination of white wine, tomatoes and basil is an Italian classic, so it seems in the spirit of the recipe to use an Italian wine like Pinot Grigio, but any crisp dry white will do. Serve with some boiled rice or crisp fried courgettes/zucchini for a deliciously light, quick supper dish for two.

3 tablespoons olive oil
200 g/7 oz. raw tiger prawns/
  shrimp, thawed if frozen
1 small onion or 2 shallots,
  very finely chopped
1 garlic clove, crushed
100 ml/⅓ cup plus 1
  tablespoon Pinot Grigio or
  other crisp dry white wine
350 g/12 oz. vine-ripened
  tomatoes, skins removed*,
  then roughly chopped
a small pinch of sugar
8 fresh basil leaves, torn
sea salt and freshly ground
  black pepper
boiled rice, to serve

Serves 2

Heat 2 tablespoons oil in a frying pan/skillet or wok, add the prawns/shrimp and fry briefly until they turn pink. Remove them from the pan with a slotted spoon and set aside.

Add the remaining oil to the pan, then add the onion or shallots and fry for 1–2 minutes until softened but not browned. Stir in the garlic, then pour in the wine and cook until it has almost evaporated. Add the tomatoes and their juice and cook for 4–5 minutes, breaking them up with a fork or spatula to make a thick sauce. Add the sugar, season to taste with salt and pepper, then stir in the basil leaves. Return the prawns/shrimp and any accumulated juices to the pan and heat through gently. Serve immediately with boiled rice.

*To remove the skins from the tomatoes, cut a cross in the bottom of each one using a small, sharp knife. Put the tomatoes in a heatproof bowl and cover them with boiling water. Let stand for about 1 minute, then remove them with a slotted spoon. When cool enough to handle, peel off the skins.

What to drink

A glass of the same wine used to make the dish – preferably a crisp dry Italian white, such as Pinot Grigio.

Hot buttered crab dip

Brown crab meat often gets overlooked by fresher-tasting white meat but it has an incredible richness which makes it a great base for bisques and dips. And it LOVES Amontillado sherry. If you have some crab in the freezer this is a great storecupboard standby.

2 tablespoons Amontillado sherry

75 g/¹/₃ cup unsalted butter, cut into cubes

450 g/1 lb. brown crab meat

2 tablespoons grated Parmesan

a good pinch of mace

cayenne pepper

a squeeze of lemon

Serves 4

Measure the sherry into a pan and add the cubed butter. Gently melt over a low heat then stir in the crab meat. Heat through to just under boiling point and simmer for a couple of minutes then take off the heat and season to taste with mace (go easy, it's powerful), cayenne pepper and a squeeze of lemon. (You probably won't need salt.)

Pour into warmed ramekin dishes, sprinkle lightly with cayenne pepper and serve with toast fingers or pitta crisps/chips.

What to drink

You could serve sherry but I'd personally go for a rich white like a Chardonnay or a Godello.

Roast monkfish with pancetta, rosemary and red wine gravy

Monkfish makes an excellent alternative to a meaty roast, especially when it is served with a robust red wine gravy. It also makes an impressive main course for a dinner party.

8 sprigs of rosemary

7 garlic cloves

50 g/3¹/₂ tablespoons butter at room temperature, plus an extra 25 g/1³/₄ tablespoons, chilled and cut into cubes

2 small monkfish tails, about 450 g/16 oz. each, skinned, boned and each divided into 2 fillets

110 g/4 oz. very thinly sliced pancetta or dry-cure streaky/fatty bacon, rind removed

2 tablespoons olive oil

8 shallots, quartered

175 ml/³/₄ cup full-bodied fruity red wine, such as Merlot or Argentinian Malbec

125 ml/¹/₂ cup light chicken or vegetable stock

sea salt and freshly ground black pepper

sautéed potatoes, to serve

mixed leaf salad, to serve

Serves 4–6

What to drink

A Merlot or a Sangiovese or Sangiovese-based Italian red.

Strip the leaves from four of the rosemary sprigs, chop them very finely and transfer to a bowl. Crush one garlic clove and add it to the rosemary along with the softened butter. Season with a little salt and pepper and beat well with a wooden spoon.

Preheat the oven to 200°C (400°F) Gas 6.

Lay out the monkfish fillets in pairs with the thin end of one fillet next to the thick end of the other. Spread the rosemary and garlic butter over one side of each fillet, then press each pair together with the buttered sides in the middle. Wrap the slices of pancetta or bacon around each pair of fillets, enclosing them completely. Put 1 tablespoon of the olive oil in a shallow cast-iron pan (or another flameproof dish that you can later put over a burner), then add the wrapped monkfish. Put the remaining garlic cloves, rosemary sprigs and shallots around the monkfish, then drizzle over the remaining oil. Roast the monkfish in the preheated oven for 25 minutes, turning the shallots and garlic halfway through, until the pancetta or bacon is nicely browned.

Carefully remove the monkfish from the pan, lightly cover with foil and set aside. Leaving the shallots and garlic in the pan, pour off all but 1 tablespoon of the oil and butter, then put the pan over a medium heat. Heat the contents of the pan for a couple of minutes, stirring, then pour in the wine. Let it bubble up and reduce by half, then add the stock. Continue to let it bubble until the liquid is reduced by half again. Strain the gravy through a fine-meshed sieve/strainer and return it to the pan, along with any juices that have accumulated from the fish. Reheat gently, then whisk in the chilled butter. Check the seasoning – it may need a little pepper.

Cut the monkfish fillets into thick slices, divide them among four or six plates and spoon over a little red wine gravy. Serve with sautéed potatoes and a mixed leaf salad.

Hake with sherry and garlic chips

This may sound like an alarming amount of garlic but the slow cooking reduces its pungency and makes it taste deliciously sweet. Do buy fresh garlic though. Garlic that's been kept for a while can develop a bitter taste.

3 tablespoons olive oil plus 1 teaspoon

5 garlic cloves (about half a head of garlic), peeled and finely sliced

200 g/7 oz. purple sprouting broccoli

3 tablespoons fino sherry

3–4 tablespoons fish or vegetable stock

a handful of flat leaf parsley leaves, stripped off the stalk

a good pinch of Turkish dried chilli flakes/red pepper flakes

2 x 175-g/6-oz. hake fillets

sea salt and freshly ground black pepper

sautéed potatoes, to serve (optional)

Serves 2

Heat 3 tablespoons of the olive oil in a small frying pan/skillet over a moderate heat. Add the sliced garlic cloves and once they begin to sizzle, reduce the heat and cook over a medium to low heat until lightly browned.

While the garlic is cooking, steam the broccoli lightly until just cooked and set aside.

Pour the sherry into the garlic, bubble up and then add the stock, parsley leaves and a pinch of sea salt and dried chilli/red pepper flakes. Simmer for a couple of minutes and then pour into a small bowl. Wipe the pan with a paper towel and add the remaining teaspoon of olive oil. Seasons the hake lightly with salt and pepper and place each fillet skin-side down in the olive oil. Fry for 3–4 minutes until the skin is crisp and the fish just over half-cooked. Turn the fillets over and cook on the other side for about 30 seconds to 1 minute.

Place the hake fillets on warm plates with the broccoli on the side, warm through the oil and garlic and pour it over the hake and the broccoli. You could also serve some sautéed potatoes on the side.

What to drink

The fino sherry you use for the recipe should go really well or try an oak-aged white Rioja or Douro white from northern Portugal.

Fine wine fish pie with salmon and scallops

Some dishes are worth making just because they show off a favourite wine so well and this is one of them. It's the perfect foil for a mature white Burgundy such as a premier cru Chablis or Chassagne Montrachet.

800 g/28 oz. mashing
   potatoes, peeled and halved
   or quartered

250 g/9 oz. firm white fish
   such as cod loin, skinned

250 g/9 oz. thick salmon fillet,
   skinned

1 bay leaf

75 ml/2^1/$_2$ oz. Chablis or other
   good white Burgundy

600 ml/2^1/$_2$ cups whole/full-fat
   milk

75 g/5^1/$_3$ tablespoons butter

40 g/^{1}/$_4$ cup plain/all-purpose
   flour

200 g/7 oz. queen scallops

130 g/4^1/$_2$ oz. raw prawns/
   shrimp

2–3 tablespoons double/heavy
   cream

sea salt and fresh ground
   black or white pepper

*a medium-sized pie
   or baking dish, lightly buttered*

Serves 4–6

Cover the potatoes with cold water, bring to the boil, add salt and cook until tender.

Meanwhile place the white fish and salmon in a saucepan, add the bay leaf, pour over the wine and 550 ml/2^1/$_4$ cups of the milk and slowly bring up to simmering point. Take off the heat, remove the fish and reserve the hot wine and milk.

Heat 55 g/3^1/$_2$ tablespoons of the butter in a medium to large saucepan, stir in the flour and cook for a few seconds. Pour in the milk mixture all at once, stirring vigorously until it thickens. Leave over a low heat.

Drain the potatoes and mash until smooth. Add the remaining butter and work in well then heat the remaining milk until just below boiling and beat that in too. Check seasoning and set aside.

Preheat the oven to 200°C (400°F) Gas 6.

Add the scallops and raw prawns/shrimp to the white sauce together with any liquid in the packet and heat through. Break up the salmon and white fish into large chunks, removing any bones and fold into the sauce along with the double/heavy cream. Check the seasoning adding a dash more wine to taste if you think it needs it.

Tip the fish mixture into a lightly buttered pie or baking dish and top with the mashed potato. Place in the preheated oven for about 15 minutes until the pie is hot and the top nicely browned. You can make the pie ahead and refrigerate it in which case reheat it at 190°C (375°F) Gas 5 for 30–35 minutes.

What to drink

A fine white Burgundy such as a Chablis or Chassagne Montrachet or any top-quality creamy Chardonnay.

Sea bass en papillote with spring vegetables and fresh herbs

Baking en papillote is one of the easiest and healthiest ways of cooking fish. The fish and vegetables are laid on a large piece of foil, flavoured with a splash of wine, a knob/pat of butter and some fresh herbs, then tightly sealed so that they steam in their own juices. Light and delicious.

250 g/9 oz. mixed vegetables, such as asparagus, broccoli, courgettes/zucchini, sugar snap peas, green/French beans or baby carrots
light olive oil, for greasing
2 thick sea bass fillets, about 125 g/4¹/₂ oz. each
2 teaspoons mixed freshly chopped herbs, such as chives, chervil and dill
20 g/1¹/₂ tablespoons butter, cut into slices
4 tablespoons dry white wine, such as Pinot Grigio or Sauvignon Blanc
sea salt and freshly ground black pepper

4 large pieces of foil or parchment paper, about 28-cm/11-in. square

Serves 2

Preheat the oven to 220°C (425°F) Gas 7.

Chop the vegetables into large, even-sized pieces. Lay out two pieces of foil or parchment paper one on top of the other and grease the top layer lightly with a few drops of olive oil. Lay one sea bass fillet on it and surround it with half the vegetables. Sprinkle with half the herbs, dot with half the butter and season with salt and pepper. Pull up the sides of the foil or parchment paper and add 2 tablespoons wine to the parcel. Carefully pull the sides together around the fish and vegetables, leaving a space around them, but sealing the parcel tightly at the top so the juices can't escape. Repeat with the remaining ingredients to make a second parcel.

Put the two parcels on a baking sheet and bake in the preheated oven for 12 minutes. Remove the parcels from the oven and open them carefully. Transfer the fish and vegetables to two warm plates, pour over the juices and serve immediately.

What to drink

A classic French wine, such as Chablis or Sancerre would respect the delicate flavours of this dish. Or try a Spanish Albariño.

Meat and poultry

Burgundy-style pork with white wine and mustard sauce

This typical wine, cream and mustard sauce from Burgundy is quick, easy and versatile. You could equally well use it for chicken.

1 tablespoon olive oil
15 g/⅛ stick butter
2 boneless pork loin
   steaks, approx.
   150–160 g/5–6 oz. each
125 g/2 cups chestnut
   mushrooms, rinsed
   and thickly sliced
1 teaspoon plain/
   all-purpose flour
100 ml/⅓ cup plus
   1 tablespoon white
   Burgundy or other dry
   white wine

1 teaspoon freshly
   chopped thyme leaves
2 tablespoons crème
   fraîche
2 rounded teaspoons
   wholegrain mustard
sea salt and freshly
   ground black pepper
1 tablespoon freshly
   snipped chives, boiled
   new potatoes and
   green salad, to serve

Serves 2

Heat the oil and butter in a medium frying pan/skillet. Add the pork steaks and brown them for about 3 minutes on each side. Reduce the heat and cook for a further 2–3 minutes on each side or until cooked through. Remove the pork steaks from the pan, set aside and keep them warm.

Add the mushrooms to the pan and cook for about 5 minutes until lightly browned. Scoop them out with a slotted spoon, add to the pork and keep warm. Using a wooden spoon, stir the flour into the juices in the pan. Stir in the wine and thyme leaves and let bubble up until reduced by about two-thirds. Reduce the heat to very low, then stir in the crème fraîche and mustard. Heat very gently, taking care not to let the sauce boil or the mustard will taste bitter. Season to taste with salt and pepper.

Return the pork, mushrooms and any juices to the pan and heat through very gently. To serve, put the pork steaks on two warm plates, spoon the sauce over the top, sprinkle with a few snipped chives and accompany with new potatoes and a green salad.

What to drink

Chablis would go very well with this dish, as would a young red Burgundy.

Chicken with chardonnay and chanterelles

This dish is perfect for a romantic dinner for two, therefore it's worth using a really good wine to make it. You need only a glass for cooking the chicken, so the rest of the bottle can be drunk with the meal.

15 g/¹/₃ cup dried chanterelles

1 tablespoon plain/all-purpose flour

2 boneless chicken breasts, about 350 g/12 oz.

2 tablespoons olive oil

35 g/2 tablespoons plus 1 teaspoon butter

4 shallots, thinly sliced

a good pinch of Spanish sweet smoked paprika (pimentòn)

150 ml/²/₃ cup top-quality New World Chardonnay or good white Burgundy

3 tablespoons double/heavy cream

2 coils dried pappardelle all'uovo or other wide-ribboned egg pasta, about 100 g/3¹/₂ oz.

freshly grated nutmeg

1 tablespoon freshly chopped parsley

sea salt and freshly ground black pepper

an ovenproof dish

Serves 2

What to drink
_____

The rest of the bottle you used in the recipe.

Soak the chanterelles. Drain the chanterelles, reserve the soaking liquid and strain it through a fine sieve/strainer.

Preheat the oven to 200°C (400°F) Gas 6.

Put the flour in a shallow dish and season it with salt and pepper. Dip the chicken breasts into the flour and coat both sides. Heat a medium frying pan/skillet over moderate heat, add 1 tablespoon olive oil and 10 g/ 2 teaspoons butter. When the butter is foaming, add the chicken breasts skin-side down. Fry for 2¹/₂–3 minutes until the skin is brown and crisp. Turn the chicken over and lightly brown the other side for 2¹/₂–3 minutes. Transfer the chicken to an ovenproof dish and cook in the preheated oven for 15–20 minutes until cooked.

Meanwhile, discard the fat from the frying pan/skillet and wipe the pan with paper towels. Heat the remaining oil and 15 g/1 tablespoon butter in the pan, add the shallots and fry gently for 5–6 minutes or until soft. Stir in the paprika, then increase the heat to high and add the wine. When the wine has reduced by half, add 90 ml/¹/₃ cup of the reserved mushroom water. Reduce the heat and let simmer gently for 10 minutes. Strain the sauce through a fine sieve/strainer into a heatproof bowl. Return the strained sauce to the pan, add the chanterelles, cover and simmer for 10 minutes.

Remove the pan from the heat, stir in the cream and salt and pepper to taste. Return the pan to the burner and heat very gently, stirring occasionally, until the sauce thickens.

To cook the pasta, bring a large saucepan of lightly salted water to the boil, add the pasta and cook until al dente. Drain well, add the remaining butter and season with pepper and freshly grated nutmeg.

Cut each chicken breast into five or six thick diagonal slices. Divide the pasta between two warm plates, put the slices of chicken on top, then spoon over the mushroom and cream sauce. Sprinkle with chopped parsley and serve immediately.

Slow-braised lamb shanks with red wine, rosemary and garlic

The preparation and cooking of this dish can be spread over three days, which makes it the perfect dish for Sunday lunch.

6 even-sized lamb shanks, about 2 kg/4¹/₂ lbs. in total

1 large onion, thinly sliced

3 carrots, cut into thin batons

4 garlic cloves, thinly sliced

2–3 sprigs of rosemary

¹/₂ teaspoon black peppercorns

1 bottle robust red wine, 750 ml/3¹/₄ cups, such as Shiraz, Malbec or Zinfandel, plus 75 ml/¹/₃ cup extra to finish

4 tablespoons olive oil

500 ml/2 cups passata/ strained tomatoes

tomato ketchup, to taste

sea salt and freshly ground black pepper

creamy mashed potatoes and green/French beans, to serve

a large heavyweight plastic bag

a large lidded flameproof casserole

Serves 6

Put the lamb shanks in a large, heavyweight plastic bag. Add the onion, carrots, garlic, rosemary and peppercorns. Pour in the bottle of wine, then pull up the sides of the bag so the marinade covers the meat. Secure the top of the bag with a wire twist. Put the bag in a bowl or dish and refrigerate overnight. The next day, remove the lamb shanks from the marinade, pat them dry with paper towels and season with salt and pepper. Strain the marinade through a sieve/strainer into a large bowl and reserve the vegetables.

Preheat the oven to 170°C (325°F) Gas 3.

Heat half the oil in a large flameproof casserole, add the lamb shanks and brown them thoroughly on all sides – you may need to do this in two batches. Remove the lamb and set it aside. Add the remaining oil to the casserole, then add the reserved vegetables and fry briefly until they begin to soften. Add a few tablespoons of the marinade and let it bubble up, incorporating any caramelized juices that have stuck to the casserole. Stir in the passata/strained tomatoes and the rest of the marinade, then return the lamb shanks to the pan. Spoon the vegetables and sauce over the lamb and bring to simmering point. Cover the meat tightly with parchment paper, put the lid on the casserole and cook in the preheated oven for 1³/₄–2 hours until the meat is almost tender.

Remove the lid and paper and cook for a further 30 minutes. Remove the rosemary sprigs, let cool, cover and refrigerate overnight.

The next day, carefully remove any fat that has accumulated on the surface. Reheat gently on the top of the stove until the sauce comes to simmering point. If the sauce isn't thick enough, remove the lamb shanks from the pan, simmer the sauce until it thickens, then return the lamb to the pan. Add the remaining wine and simmer for a further 15 minutes. Season to taste with salt and pepper and sweeten with a little tomato ketchup, if necessary. Serve with creamy mashed potatoes and green/French beans.

What to drink

Drink a similar wine to the one you've used to make the dish. A Malbec would be perfect.

Venison sausages with red wine and rosemary gravy

This is real comfort food, poshed up for a dinner party. Rosemary works really well with red wine in a gravy. Easy to make. Everyone will love it. Win, win!

600 g/21 oz. venison sausages

FOR THE GRAVY
4 tablespoons light olive oil
20 g/1¹/₂ tablespoons butter
2 medium red onions, thinly sliced
2 garlic cloves, crushed
1 tablespoon freshly chopped rosemary leaves
1 tablespoon tomato purée/paste
1 tablespoon plain/ all-purpose flour
175 ml/³/₄ cup full-bodied red wine
175 ml/³/₄ cup beef stock
sea salt and freshly ground black pepper
mashed or baked potatoes and red cabbage, to serve

Serves 4

Heat a frying pan/skillet over a moderate heat. Add 2 tablespoons of the oil, heat for 1 minute then add the butter.

Once the butter has melted tip in the onions, stir and cook over a moderate heat until they start to brown. Add the crushed garlic and rosemary, stir and cook for another minute. Add the tomato purée/paste, stir, cook for a minute and then work in the flour.

Pour in the red wine and beef stock, bring to the boil, season lightly with salt and a generous amount of freshly ground black pepper then turn the heat right down and simmer for 15 minutes. Check the seasoning and adjust to taste.

Meanwhile brown the sausages well on all sides in the remaining oil. Drain off the fat and add the sausages to the gravy. Leave over a low heat for 10 minutes or so for the sausages to absorb some of the sauce then serve with mashed or baked potatoes. Red cabbage is also delicious with this dish.

What to drink

A hearty red such as a Malbec or Shiraz.

Entrecôte Marchand de Vin

One of the great French classics, Entrecôte Marchand de Vin (wine merchant's steak) is cooked in a simple red wine sauce. I say simple, but I actually think it's worth using a seriously good wine and drinking the rest of the bottle with it. It's usually made with red Bordeaux, but I also like to use a good, but not too oaky, Syrah or Shiraz.

2 entrecôte or sirloin steaks, 225 g/8 oz. each and 2 cm/³/4 in. thick, trimmed of excess fat
1 tablespoon olive oil
40 g/3 tablespoons butter, softened
2 shallots, very finely chopped
125 ml/¹/2 cup good-quality red wine, such as Bordeaux, Syrah or Shiraz

2 rounded tablespoons freshly chopped flat leaf parsley
sea salt and freshly ground black pepper
sautéed potatoes and a mixed leaf salad, to serve

Serves 2

Pat the steaks dry with paper towels. Heat a heavy-based frying pan/skillet over a medium to high heat for about 2 minutes. Add the olive oil and, when it is hot, add 15 g/1 tablespoon of the butter. Wait until the foaming subsides, then put the steaks in the pan. Cook for 3 minutes, then turn and cook for another 2–3 minutes for a medium-rare steak. Transfer to a warm plate and cover lightly with aluminium foil.

Discard the fat in the pan and add half the remaining butter. Once it has melted, add the shallots and cook over a low heat for about 2 minutes. Increase the heat, pour in the wine and let bubble away for 2–3 minutes until it has reduced by about two-thirds. Gradually whisk in the remaining butter, pour in any juices that have accumulated under the steak and stir. Season with salt and pepper, then add the parsley.

Serve the steaks with the sauce poured over, accompanied by sautéed potatoes and mixed salad leaves.

What to drink

A classic French dish which provides the perfect excuse to crack open a good bottle of Bordeaux.

Pork, pancetta and polpettine

This is a lemony, creamy riff on spaghetti and meatballs though they taste equally good with rice.

50 g/2 oz. 2-day-old white or sourdough bread, torn into chunks

25 g/³/4 oz. Parmesan, plus extra for serving

2 large garlic cloves

50 g/2 oz. pancetta or guanciale, chopped

40 g/1¹/2 oz. flat leaf parsley, plus extra for serving

450 g/1 lb. lean minced/ground pork or veal

grated rind of 1 lemon

1 egg yolk

2 tablespoons olive oil

30 g/2¹/2 tablespoons butter

100 ml/¹/3 cup plus 1 tablespoon dry Italian white wine

1 medium onion, finely chopped

150 g/³/4 cup ripe tomatoes, skinned and roughly chopped

1 tablespoon flour, plus extra for dusting the polpettine

250 ml/1 cup plus 1 tablespoon chicken stock

3 tablespoons double/heavy cream

sea salt and freshly ground black pepper, to taste

pasta or rice, to serve

Serves 4 (makes 20–24 meatballs)

Put the bread in a food processor with the Parmesan, roughly broken into chunks, 1 roughly chopped garlic clove, the chopped pancetta and just under half the parsley. Pulse until the mixture gets to breadcrumb consistency, then add the minced/ground pork or veal, half the grated lemon rind, egg yolk, salt and pepper and pulse again. Leave for 15 minutes then take dessert spoons, and roll the mixture into meatballs with floured hands.

Heat 1 tablespoon of the oil, add half the butter and fry the meatballs on all sides until lightly browned. Remove from the pan with a slotted spoon, pour off any excess fat and deglaze the pan with half the wine. Pour over the meatballs.

Heat the remaining oil in the pan, add the remaining butter and sauté the onion over a low heat until soft. Crush the remaining garlic clove, add to the pan and stir. Turn the heat up, add the tomatoes and cook until they start to break down. Add the remaining wine, cook until evaporated and stir in the flour. Add the chicken stock and bring up to simmering point. Tip in the meatballs, turn them in the sauce and leave over a low heat while you cook the rice or pasta. Add a spoonful of the pasta cooking water to the sauce.

Stir the remaining chopped parsley into the meatballs and check the seasoning. Swirl in the cream and serve the meatballs over the pasta or rice, sprinkling with the rest of the parsley. Serve extra Parmesan on the side.

What to drink

A dry Italian white wine such as a Verdicchio.

Languedoc beef stew with red wine, herbs and olives

*This adaptation of the classic French daube was always one of
my favourite dishes to make at our holiday home in France. Of course
I use the delicious local red Faugères wine, but you could use any
robust fruity red. Note that I add a little extra wine right at the end
– it lifts the winey flavour after the long, slow cooking.*

1 kg/2¼ lb. thickly sliced
  braising or stewing steak
25 g/3 tablespoons plain/
  all-purpose flour
5–6 tablespoons olive oil
1 large onion, thinly sliced
2 large garlic cloves, crushed
1 tablespoon tomato purée/
  paste
300 ml/1¼ cups Faugères
  or other full-bodied fruity
  red wine
125 ml/½ cup fresh beef stock
1 teaspoon herbes de Provence
1 thin strip of orange zest
2 bay leaves
100 g/1 cup black olives
3 heaped tablespoons roughly
  chopped flat leaf parsley
sea salt and freshly ground
  black pepper

**FOR THE SLOW-ROASTED
CARROTS**
500 g/18 oz. carrots
a pinch of cayenne pepper
2 tablespoons olive oil

a cast-iron casserole

a large, shallow ovenproof dish

Serves 4–6

Trim any excess fat from the beef, then cut the meat into large cubes. Put the flour in a shallow dish and season it with salt and pepper. Dip the cubes of beef in the flour to coat.

Heat 2 tablespoons oil in a large frying pan/skillet, add the beef and fry on all sides until it is browned – you will need to do this in batches, adding extra oil as you go. Transfer the beef to a cast-iron casserole.

Heat the remaining oil in the frying pan/skillet, add the onion and cook for 3–4 minutes until softened but not browned. Add the garlic and tomato purée/paste and cook for 1 minute, stirring. Add 250 ml/1 cup plus 1 tablespoon of the wine, the stock, herbes de Provence, orange zest and bay leaves. Bring to the boil, then pour the sauce into the casserole. Heat the casserole over a medium heat and bring the sauce back to the boil. Reduce the heat, cover and simmer very gently for 2½–3 hours until the meat is completely tender. Check the contents of the casserole occasionally to ensure there is enough liquid (add a little extra stock or water if it's too dry).

Preheat the oven to 180°C (350°F) Gas 4. About two-thirds of the way through the cooking time, prepare the slow-roasted carrots. Cut the carrots into long, thick diagonal slices. Put the carrots, salt and cayenne pepper in a large ovenproof dish, pour over the oil and toss well. Bake in the preheated oven for about 45 minutes until the carrots are soft and their edges caramelized.

About 30 minutes before the stew is cooked, stir in the olives. Just before serving, season to taste with salt and pepper, then stir in the parsley and the remaining wine and cook for a further 5 minutes. Serve with the slow-roasted carrots.

What to drink

Try a Faugères or other full-bodied Languedoc red.

Sautéed chicken with white wine, pea and tarragon sauce

This is one of the easiest supper dishes imaginable. It takes less time to cook than a ready meal and it is much more delicious. You can use any dry white wine to make it, but I particularly like the richness of Viognier, an exotic, slightly scented grape variety that thrives in southern France and, nowadays, in Australia and California, too. Unoaked or lightly oaked Chardonnay will also work well.

1 tablespoon olive oil

100 g/3¹/₂ oz. pancetta cubes or dry-cured streaky/fatty bacon, chopped

2 skinless, boneless chicken breasts, cut into thin slices

1 small onion, very finely chopped

125 ml/¹/₂ cup full-bodied dry white wine, such as Viognier

150 g/1 cup fresh podded or frozen peas

2 tablespoons freshly chopped tarragon leaves

100 g/4 rounded tablespoons crème fraîche/sour cream

freshly ground black pepper

steamed asparagus tips, to serve

Serves 2

Heat the oil in a large frying pan/skillet, then add the pancetta cubes or bacon. Fry for a couple of minutes until the fat starts to run. Add the chicken slices and fry, stirring occasionally, until lightly golden, around 4–5 minutes.

Add the onion to the pan and fry for 1–2 minutes. Add the wine and peas and cook until the wine has reduced by about two-thirds. Reduce the heat and stir in the tarragon, crème fraîche/sour cream and black pepper, to taste. Heat gently until almost bubbling.

Remove the pan from the heat. Transfer the sautéed chicken to two warm plates, spoon over the sauce and serve with steamed asparagus tips.

What to drink

Serve a glass of the wine used to make the dish – a Viognier or an unoaked or lightly oaked Chardonnay.

Rabbit with mustard
(Lapin à la moutarde)

This is the kind of classic old-fashioned bistro dish you used to get all over France (now you're more likely to find pizza, sadly). Still, you can make it at home and it's delicious. If you prefer not to eat rabbit you can substitute chicken – thighs would be the ideal cut.

2 tablespoons seasoned plain/all-purpose flour

3 tablespoons olive oil

20 g/1½ tablespoons butter

1 medium-sized rabbit, cut into 6 pieces

75 g/2¾ oz. lardons or pancetta cubes

1 medium onion, finely chopped

1 garlic clove, crushed

1 teaspoon freshly chopped thyme

100 ml/⅓ cup plus 1 tablespoon dry white wine, such as Chablis or Aligoté

125 ml/½ cup chicken stock, preferably home-made

2–3 tablespoons wholegrain mustard

2–3 tablespoons crème fraîche/sour cream

2 tablespoons freshly chopped chives or parsley

sea salt and freshly ground black pepper

tagliatelle or boiled new potatoes, to serve

Serves 4–6

Put the flour in a shallow dish and lightly coat the rabbit pieces. Heat 2 tablespoons of the olive oil, add the butter and fry the rabbit pieces on all sides until nicely browned.

Remove the rabbit from the pan. Add another tablespoon of oil to the pan and fry the lardons and onion until the onion is soft. Add the crushed garlic and thyme, stir, then pour in the white wine, stock, and 2 tablespoons of the mustard.

Bring back up to simmering point and return the rabbit pieces to the pan, cover and cook over a low heat for about 45 minutes until tender.

Add the remaining mustard if you feel it needs it (I generally do) and 2–3 tablespoons of crème fraîche/sour cream and reheat gently – you don't want it to simmer this time. Sprinkle with the chopped chives or parsley and serve with tagliatelle or boiled new potatoes and a green salad.

What to drink

The same sort of white wine you use to make the dish. Chablis is ideal.

Spiced chicken with cardamom and viognier

It may not be orthodox to put wine into what is basically a korma but it works remarkably well, as does the almond butter which gives the dish a rich, creamy texture. If you need to make it dairy-free leave out the cream and add coconut milk.

4–6 skinless, boneless chicken breasts
3 tablespoons vegetable oil
2 medium onions, finely chopped
3 large garlic cloves, peeled and crushed
20 g/³/₄ oz. ginger, peeled and grated (a microplane works particularly well for this)
1 teaspoon garam masala
12 cardamom pods
1 bay leaf
a pinch of ground chilli/chile powder
¹/₂ teaspoon ground turmeric
60 ml/¹/₄ cup Viognier or Chardonnay
3 tablespoons almond butter
200 ml/1 scant cup chicken stock
15 g/¹/₃ cup coriander/cilantro leaves
25 g/1 oz. toasted flaked/slivered almonds
75 ml/¹/₃ cup double/heavy cream or Greek yogurt
1 mild green chilli/chile, deseeded and finely sliced (optional)
salt
rice, to serve

Serves 4

Cut the chicken breasts into three if large or in half if smaller. Heat the oil in a shallow sauté pan and fry the chicken pieces on both sides until lightly coloured. Remove from the pan with a slotted spoon.

Add the chopped onions to the pan and cook over a moderate heat until soft and beginning to brown. Add the crushed garlic and grated ginger, stir and cook for a couple of minutes. Add the garam masala, cardamom pods, bay leaf, chilli/chile and turmeric, stir and cook for a minute then add the Viognier and cook until almost evaporated. Stir in the almond butter. Add the stock and stir until the sauce thickens then return the chicken pieces to the pan. Turn them over in the sauce, put a lid on the pan and leave over a very low heat while you cook some rice. Check the seasoning and remove any cardamom pods you can spot.

Stir in half of the flaked/slivered almonds and most of the coriander/cilantro leaves, leaving some to sprinkle over the finished plates. Stir the cream into the sauce. Serve the chicken with rice, sprinkling each portion with a few almonds, coriander/cilantro leaves and slices of chilli/chile for those who want them (or serve the latter separately).

What to drink

The Viognier or Chardonnay you use to make the dish.

Italian-style roast pork with white wine, garlic and fennel

This is one of my favourite family recipes for the weekend. You can leave it for hours gently bubbling away in the oven and you will have a fantastic dish at the end of the day. I generally use an Italian wine like a Pinot Grigio, but you could use any dry white wine.

3 kg/6¹/₂ lb. boned, rolled pork shoulder/butt

2 tablespoons fennel seeds

1 tablespoon coarse sea salt

1 teaspoon black peppercorns

1 teaspoon crushed dried chillies/chiles

6 large garlic cloves, roughly chopped

freshly squeezed juice of 2 lemons

2 tablespoons olive oil

175 ml/3/4 cup dry white wine

sautéed potatoes and salad or mashed potatoes and green beans, to serve

a large roasting pan with a rack

an ovenproof dish

Serves 8

Preheat the oven to 200°C (400°F) Gas 6.

Cut deep slits in the pork skin with a sharp knife. Grind the fennel seeds, salt, peppercorns and chillies/chiles using a pestle and mortar. Add the chopped garlic and pound to a rough paste. Using your hands, smother the paste all over the pork working it into the slits. Put the pork on a wire rack and place it over a roasting pan. Cook, skin-side up in the preheated oven for 25–30 minutes. Remove the pork from the oven and reduce the heat to 120°C (250°F) Gas ¹/₂. Turn the pork over and pour half the lemon juice and all of the olive oil over it. Return the pork to the oven and cook for at least 7 hours, checking it every couple of hours. You should be aware that the meat is cooking – it should be sizzling quietly. Ovens vary, so you may want to increase the temperature slightly.

About halfway through the cooking time, spoon off the excess fat and squeeze the remaining lemon juice over the meat. About 30 minutes before the pork is due to be cooked, remove it from the oven and increase the heat to 220°C (425°F) Gas 7. Transfer the pork, skin-side up, to a clean ovenproof dish and, when the oven is hot, return the pork to the oven for about 15 minutes to crisp up the crackling. Remove from the oven and let rest.

Pour off any excess fat from the original roasting pan and add the wine and 175 ml/3/4 cup water. Heat gently on the top of the stove, working off any sticky burnt-on bits from the edges of the pan and simmer for 10 minutes. Strain the juices through a sieve/strainer and keep them warm. Carve the pork into thick slices. Put a few slices on each of eight warmed plates and pour some of the pan juices over the top. You could serve this with sautéed potatoes and salad or mashed potatoes and green beans.

What to drink

If you want to stick to white, a quality Pinot Grigio or Italian Soave would be perfect with this dish. Or try a Chianti Classico.

Duck casserole with red wine, cinnamon and olives

Red wine and cinnamon are natural partners and work together brilliantly in this exotically spiced, Moorish-style casserole. I suggest you use a strong, fruity wine such as a Merlot, Carmenère or Zinfandel.

2 duck breasts

4 duck legs

3 tablespoons olive oil

1 medium onion, thinly sliced

1 celery stalk, thinly sliced

1 garlic clove, crushed

350 ml/1¹/₂ cups full-bodied fruity red wine (see recipe introduction), plus 2 tablespoons extra

250 ml/1 cup passata/strained tomatoes

2 small strips of unwaxed orange zest

1 cinnamon stick

100 g/1 cup pitted mixed olives marinated with herbs

¹/₂ teaspoon herbes de Provence or dried oregano

sea salt and freshly ground black pepper

couscous or pilaf and leafy green vegetables, to serve

an ovenproof dish

Serves 4

Preheat the oven to 200°C (400°F) Gas 6.

Trim any excess fat from all the duck pieces and prick the skin with a fork. Cut the breasts in half lengthways and season all the pieces lightly with salt and pepper. Put 1 tablespoon oil in an ovenproof dish and add the duck pieces, skin-side upwards. Roast in the preheated oven for 20 minutes, then remove from the oven and pour off the fat (keep it for roasting potatoes). Reduce the oven temperature to 150°C (300°F) Gas 2.

Meanwhile, heat the remaining oil in a flameproof casserole, add the onion and celery and fry over a low heat for 5–6 minutes or until soft. Stir in the garlic, increase the heat and pour in the red wine. Simmer for 1–2 minutes, then add the passata/strained tomatoes, orange zest, cinnamon, olives and herbs. Transfer the duck pieces to the casserole and spoon the sauce over them. Bring the sauce to a simmer, cover and transfer the casserole to the preheated oven for about 1¹/₄ hours until the duck is tender. Spoon the sauce over the duck halfway through cooking and add a little water if the sauce seems too dry.

Take the casserole out of the oven, remove and discard the cinnamon stick and orange zest and spoon off any fat that has accumulated on the surface. Stir in 2 tablespoons red wine and season to taste with salt and pepper. Serve with couscous or a lightly spiced pilaf along with some cavolo nero or other dark leafy greens.

Note: You can also make this casserole a day ahead. To do so, cook it in the oven for just 1 hour, then let it cool, cover and refrigerate overnight. The following day, skim off any fat, then reheat it gently, adding a final dash of wine just before serving.

What to drink

Any robust southern French, Spanish, Portuguese or southern Italian red would go well with this recipe. As would a good, gutsy Zinfandel.

Coq au vin

*This classic French recipe is a terrific dish for a dinner party
The French would always use a local wine to make it – I'd suggest
a good Côtes du Rhône-Villages, a Gigondas or Lirac.*

300 g/10½ oz. shallots

3 tablespoons plain/
  all-purpose flour

6 large skinless, boneless
  chicken breasts

3 tablespoons olive oil

125 g/4½ oz. chopped streaky/
  fatty bacon or pancetta cubes

2 garlic cloves, thinly sliced

50 ml/3½ tablespoons brandy

3 sprigs of thyme

1 bay leaf

1 bottle dry fruity red wine
  750 ml/3¼ cups (see recipe
  introduction)

250 g/3½ cups small button
  mushrooms

15 g/1 tablespoon butter,
  softened (optional)

3 tablespoons freshly chopped
  flat leaf parsley

sea salt and freshly ground
  black pepper

creamy mashed potatoes
  or tagliatelle, to serve

Serves 6

What to drink

Drink a similar wine to
that you've used to make the
dish. Say, a Côtes du Rhone-
Villages or a Gigondas.

Cut the shallots into even-sized pieces, leaving the small ones whole and halving or quartering the others.

Put 2 tablespoons of flour in a shallow dish and season it with salt and pepper. Dip the chicken breasts in the flour and coat both sides. Heat 2 tablespoons olive oil in a large lidded frying pan/skillet or deep flameproof casserole, add the chicken breasts and fry for 2–3 minutes on each side until lightly browned – you may have to do this in two batches.

Remove the chicken from the pan, discard the oil and wipe the pan with kitchen paper. Return the pan to the heat and pour in the remaining oil. Add the chopped bacon or pancetta cubes and the shallots and fry until lightly browned. Stir in the garlic, then return the chicken to the pan. Put the brandy in a small saucepan and heat it until almost boiling. Set it alight with a long cook's match or taper and carefully pour it over the chicken. Let the flames die down, then add the thyme and bay leaf and pour in enough wine to just cover the chicken. Bring back to simmering point, then reduce the heat, half-cover the pan and simmer very gently for 45 minutes. (If you're making this dish ahead of time, take the pan off the heat after 30 minutes, let cool and refrigerate overnight.) Add the mushrooms to the pan and cook for another 10–15 minutes. Remove the chicken from the pan, set aside and keep it warm. Using a slotted spoon, scoop the shallots, bacon pieces or pancetta cubes and mushrooms out of the pan and keep them warm. Increase the heat under the pan and let the sauce simmer until it has reduced by half. If the sauce needs thickening, mash the remaining soft butter with 1 tablespoon flour to give a smooth paste, then add it bit by bit to the sauce, whisking well after each addition, until the sauce is smooth and glossy.

Return the shallots, pancetta and mushrooms to the pan. Check the seasoning and add salt and pepper, to taste. Cut each chicken breast into four slices and arrange them on warm serving plates. Spoon a generous amount of sauce over the chicken and sprinkle with parsley. Serve with creamy mashed potatoes or tagliatelle.

Veal scallopine with marsala

This classic quick Italian dish would traditionally be made with dry (secco) Marsala but you can use sweet (dolce) Marsala if that's what you have to hand. (Add a teaspoon of sherry vinegar to correct the sweetness if you do.) You could also use medium-dry sherry. You could equally well use pork, chicken or even turkey fillets rather than veal. The key thing is to cut and beat them out thinly.

250 g/9 oz. thinly cut veal, pork or chicken fillets
1 tablespoon plain/all-purpose flour
1 tablespoon olive oil
30 g/¼ stick butter
125 g/1¾ cup button mushrooms, cleaned and thinly sliced
75 ml/⅓ cup dry Marsala or sweet Marsala with 1 teaspoon sherry vinegar
125 ml/½ cup chicken stock
½ teaspoon freshly chopped thyme
sea salt and freshly ground black pepper
your choice of pasta or sauteed potatoes and a watercress and rocket/arugula salad, to serve

Serves 2

Trim any fat off the veal and beat out thinly between a couple of sheets of baking parchment. Put the flour in a shallow dish, season with salt and pepper, and dip the veal fillets into the flour. Heat the oil, add 15 g/⅛ stick of the butter, let it foam up then tip in the sliced mushrooms.

Lightly brown then remove from the pan. Add the remaining butter and fry the veal fillets for about 2 minutes on both sides until lightly browned. Pour in the Marsala and sherry vinegar if using and bubble up then add the chicken stock and thyme and the reserved mushrooms. Cook for 3–4 minutes turning the veal and mushrooms in the sauce.

Add a little extra stock or hot water if you want to serve it with pasta (I suggest tagliatelle or fettucine). Otherwise serve with sautéed potatoes and a watercress and rocket/arugula salad.

What to drink

A slightly tricky dish as the sauce is quite rich so you don't want a wine that's too dry. Although it's not traditional I'd go for a Grenache or a GSM (Grenache, Syrah, Mourvèdre) blend.

Pepper-crusted steaks with red wine sauce

This has to be the ultimate fast-food recipe. You can make it from start to finish in 5 minutes. The red wine gives a wonderful instant sauce that takes the dish into the luxury league. After you have made this a couple of times, you'll find you won't need measurements – just pour in a dash of brandy, half a glass of red wine and a slosh of cream to finish and away you go.

1 tablespoon mixed peppercorns
$^1/_2$ teaspoon sea salt
1 teaspoon plain/all-purpose flour
2 thinly cut rump steaks, fat removed, 125–150 g/$4^1/_4$–$5^1/_2$ oz. each
1 tablespoon olive oil
25 g/$1^1/_2$ tablespoons butter
2 tablespoons brandy
75 ml/$^1/_3$ cup full-bodied fruity red wine, such as Zinfandel, Merlot or Cabernet Sauvignon

3 tablespoons fresh beef or chicken stock
1 teaspoon redcurrant jelly or a few drops of balsamic vinegar (optional)
2 tablespoons crème fraîche/sour cream
rocket/arugula salad and crusty bread, garlic mash or chips/fries, to serve

Serves 2

Put the peppercorns and salt in a mortar and pound with a pestle until coarsely ground. Tip into a shallow dish and mix in the flour. Dip each steak into the pepper mixture and press the coating in lightly, turning to coat both sides.

Heat a frying pan/skillet over a medium heat and add the oil and half the butter. Once the butter has melted, add the steaks to the pan and cook for $1^1/_2$ minutes. Turn them over and cook for 30 seconds on the other side. Transfer the steaks to 2 warm plates.

Pour the brandy into the pan and light it carefully with a long cook's match or taper. When the flames die down, add the wine and cook for a few seconds. Add the stock and simmer for 1–2 minutes. Sweeten with a little redcurrant jelly or balsamic vinegar, if you like, then stir in the crème fraîche/sour cream.

Pour the sauce over the steaks and serve with a rocket/arugula salad and some crusty bread. If you're not in a hurry, this also goes really well with garlic mash or chips/fries.

What to drink

This is the kind of dish that will take almost any medium- to full-bodied red, such as a Merlot, a Cabernet Sauvignon or a Shiraz.

Spring lamb stew (*Navarin d'agneau*)

Lamb is often associated with hearty meals but my version of this classic French stew is perfect for spring and early summer. Like most stews it benefits from being made at least a few hours ahead, if not overnight, so allow time for the stew to cool and refrigerate it so that you can remove any excess fat.

750 g/26 oz. lamb shoulder cut into large chunks or a combination of shoulder and neck

3 tablespoons seasoned plain/all-purpose flour

5 tablespoons olive oil

20 g/1½ tablespoons butter

125 ml/½ cup dry white wine

2 medium onions, sliced (sweet onions like oignons de lezignan would be ideal)

2 garlic cloves, crushed

1 teaspoon crushed coriander seeds

2–3 medium carrots, peeled and sliced

2–3 medium turnips, scrubbed and cut into even-sized cubes

2 tomatoes, peeled, deseeded and chopped

1 bay leaf

1 sprig thyme

a handful of flat leaf parsley stalks and leaves

500 ml/2 cups plus 2 tablespoons chicken or vegetable stock

400 g/3 cups new potatoes, washed

Serves 4–5

Pat the pieces of meat dry and roll in the seasoned flour. Heat a frying pan/skillet and add 2 tablespoons of the oil, then, when the oil has heated, the butter. Fry the meat on all sides a few pieces at a time. Remove from the pan and set aside.

Deglaze the pan with the wine and pour over the meat. Wipe the pan and return to the heat. Add the remaining oil, tip in the onions, stir and leave over a low heat until soft.

Add the garlic and coriander seeds then the carrots and turnips, cover and continue to cook for another 7–8 minutes, stirring occasionally. Stir in the remaining flour, tomatoes, bay leaf, thyme, whole parsley stalks and stock and bring to the boil. Add the meat, bring back to a simmer then cover and leave on a low heat or in a low 140°C (275°F) Gas 1 oven for 1½ hours, checking occasionally.

Remove from the oven, cool and refrigate. Spoon off and discard the fat, bay leaf and parsley stalks. Reheat gently. Cook the potatoes in boiling water until almost done then add to the stew. Leave over a low heat for 10 minutes for the flavours to combine, adding an extra dash of white wine if you think it needs it. Chop the parsley leaves and fold through.

You could add blanched fresh peas and skinned broad beans along with the potatoes if you like.

What to drink

You could either drink a rich white like a Viognier or an aged red wine like a mature Bordeaux or Rioja reserva with this dish.

Red-wine marinated venison

Wine doesn't have to be used for a sauce. You can simply use it as a marinade to add flavour although this recipe offers the best of both worlds: a rich-flavoured marinade and a spoonful or two of delicious cooking juices. A quick, delicious treat of a dinner for two.

2 venison fillets, 125 g/
    4¹/₂ oz. each
150 ml/²/₃ cup full-bodied red
    wine
a sprig of rosemary
2 garlic cloves, crushed
3 tablespoons beef or chicken
    stock
1 tablespoon olive oil
your choice of polenta, chips/
    fries and green leafy
    vegetables, to serve
sea salt and freshly ground
    black pepper

Serves 2

Measure 100 ml/¹/₃ cup plus 1 tablespoon of the red wine into a flat dish, add the rosemary and the crushed cloves of garlic and turn the venison fillets in the marinade. Leave to marinate for 3–4 hours turning them once.

Heat a ridged griddle pan or a heavy-bottomed frying pan/skillet for a few minutes. Remove the venison fillets from the marinade and pat dry. Rub a little oil into them then lay them onto the hot pan and cook for about 3 minutes. Turn them carefully and cook for another minute. Set the venison aside to rest for about 5 minutes.

Remove the pan from the heat and deglaze with the remaining red wine and stock. Bubble up until reduced. Check the seasoning adding salt and pepper, to taste. Serve on warm plates with polenta or chips/fries and some cavolo nero or other dark leafy greens.

What to drink

This would show off a good red wine like a red Bordeaux or similar cabernet-merlot blend.

Osso buco-style veal chops with green olive gremolata

Osso buco is one of those dishes about which huge arguments rage. Whether there should be tomato or no tomato. Whether it should be cooked for one hour or three. Well, this version gives the dish a complete makeover. It's fresher and faster, but just as delicious.

4 large veal chops, about
   1 kg/2¼ lb. in total
2 tablespoons olive oil
15 g/1 tablespoon butter
1 small onion, finely chopped
1 celery stick, thinly sliced
2 garlic cloves, crushed
150 ml/⅔ cup Italian dry white
   wine, such as Pinot Grigio
150 ml/1 cup passata rustica/
   strained tomatoes or regular
   passata
about 300 ml/1¼ cups light
   vegetable or chicken stock

**FOR THE GREEN OLIVE
GREMOLATA**
finely grated zest
   of 1 lemon
10 pitted green olives, finely
   chopped
3 heaped tablespoons freshly
   chopped parsley
your choice of saffron risotto,
   rice or green salad, to serve

Serves 4

Trim any excess fat from the chops. Heat a large shallow frying pan/skillet and add the oil. Heat for 1 minute, then add the butter. When the foaming has subsided, add the veal chops and fry them for about 3 minutes on each side until nicely browned. Remove the chops from the pan and set aside.

Add the onion and celery to the pan and cook over a low heat for 5–6 minutes until softened. Stir in the garlic, then increase the heat to high and pour in the wine. Let it bubble up for a few minutes until the wine has reduced by half, then add the passata/strained tomatoes and 225 ml/ scant 1 cup of the stock. Stir well, then return the chops to the pan, spooning the sauce over them. Bring the sauce back to a simmer, half-cover the pan and reduce the heat. Cook very gently for 30–40 minutes, turning the chops halfway through, until they are tender. If they seem to be getting dry, add a little more stock.

Meanwhile, to prepare the gremolata, put the lemon zest, chopped olives and parsley in a bowl and mix well. When the chops are ready, add half the gremolata to the pan and stir to mix. Cook over a very low heat for 5 minutes for the flavours to amalgamate.

Transfer the chops to four warm plates, spoon the sauce over the top and sprinkle with the remaining gremolata. Serve with a saffron risotto, plain boiled rice or a simple green salad.

What to drink

I'd personally drink a dry Italian white with this, such as an Orvieto or Verdicchio dei Castelli de Jesi, but you could opt for an Italian red – a Barbera, for example.

Roast chicken wings
with garlic and fino sherry

I've been making this recipe for over 20 years – originally with chicken thighs chopped in half into nuggets but these days with wings, which encourages you to eat with your fingers. A delicious tapa!

800 g/1¾ lb. chicken
   wings
1 head of garlic
3 tablespoons extra virgin
   olive oil
3 sprigs of rosemary
100 ml/⅓ cup fino sherry
sea salt and freshly ground
   black pepper

Serves 4

Preheat the oven to 180°C (350°F) Gas 4.

Chop each chicken wing in half and season generously with salt and pepper.

Heat the olive oil In a large shallow frying pan/skillet and fry the chicken wings until golden brown, turning half way through.

Separate the garlic cloves leaving the skin on and smash each clove with the flat side of a knife. Add to the pan with the rosemary and stir.

Pour in the fino sherry, bring to the boil and transfer to the oven for 30–45 minutes until the chicken is cooked and sticky with the caramelized garlic and juices. Set aside until cool enough to eat with your fingers.

What to drink

You can either drink fino as you've got a bottle open or go for an oaked white Rioja.

Spicy meatloaf with red wine-glazed onions

The deliciously sticky, spicy caramelized onion topping gives this family favourite an extra-indulgent edge. For adults only!

2 tablespoons vegetable or sunflower oil

2 medium onions, finely chopped

2 large garlic cloves, crushed

50 g/2 oz. fresh white or sourdough breadcrumbs

400 g/14 oz. sweet chilli/chile sausages or other spicy sausages

500 g/18 oz. minced/ground beef

1/4 teaspoon chilli/hot red pepper flakes (optional)

3 heaped tablespoons freshly chopped flat leaf parsley

1 small egg, beaten

FOR THE WINE-GLAZED ONIONS

3 tablespoons vegetable or sunflower oil

3 medium onions, sliced

1 teaspoon smoked paprika

25 g/2 tablespoons muscovado sugar

125 ml/1/2 cup Shiraz or other full-bodied red wine

sea salt

mashed potatoes, greens and roasted tomatoes, to serve

900-ml/4-cup loaf pan, lightly greased

Serves 4–6

Preheat the oven to 190°C (375°F) Gas 5.

First make the meatloaf. Heat the oil and fry the onions until beginning to brown. Turn the heat down and add the crushed garlic then tip into the breadcrumbs and set aside to cool. Remove the sausages from their casings and add to the breadcrumbs. Add the minced/ground beef, chilli/hot red pepper flakes if using and parsley and mix thoroughly (I find it's easiest to use your hands). Add enough beaten egg to bind, season lightly with salt and pepper (there should be a fair amount of seasoning in the sausagemeat) and mix again. Pack the mixture into the greased loaf pan and bake in the preheated oven for about 40 minutes until beginning to shrink away from the sides of the pan.

While the meatloaf is cooking make the wine-glazed onions. Heat the oil in a pan and cook the onions over a low heat until soft. Stir in the smoked paprika and sugar and a good pinch of salt, then increase the heat and cook the onions until caramelized. Add 75 ml/1/3 cup of the Shiraz and reduce until the sauce is thick. Once the meatloaf is almost cooked spread two-thirds of the onions over the top and return to the oven for about 10 minutes until they are nicely glazed. Add the rest of the wine to the remaining onions and simmer until the consistency of a rich wine gravy. Serve the meatloaf with mash, greens and roasted tomatoes with a little red wine gravy spooned over each slice.

What to drink

A fruity Shiraz or Malbec.

Vegetable dishes and pulses

Greek-style beans with mint and feta

*The Greeks have a great dish called gigantes plaki which translates
as giant baked beans. It doesn't normally appear to include wine but
I think it makes it particularly delicious.*

250 g/1½ cups Greek
  gigantes beans,
  Spanish Judion beans
  or butter beans/jumbo
  lima beans
a bay leaf
3 garlic cloves
6 peppercorns
3 tablespoons olive oil
1 large onion, finely
  sliced
¼ teaspoon cinnamon
½ teaspoon dried
  oregano
1 heaped tablespoon
  tomato purée/paste
50 ml/3½ tablespoons
  red wine, plus a dash
  extra

200 g/7 oz. canned
  chopped tomatoes
2 tablespoons flat leaf
  parsley
2 tablespoons shredded
  mint
120 g/1 cup feta cheese,
  crumbled
sea salt and freshly
  ground black pepper
Greek bread or pitta
  bread, to serve

Serves 4

Soak the beans in cold water overnight.

Preheat the oven to 150°C (300°F) Gas 2.

Drain the beans and place in a saucepan. Cover with
cold water and bring to the boil. Skim, add the bay
leaf, a peeled garlic clove and the peppercorns and
boil until tender but not falling apart which could be
anything from 45 minutes to 1 hour and 15 minutes.
Remove from the heat and drain.

Meanwhile heat the olive oil in a flameproof
casserole dish and fry the onion over a low to
medium heat until soft. Crush the remaining garlic
cloves, add them to the pan and cook for a minute
then stir in the cinnamon, oregano and tomato
purée/paste. Cook for another minute then add the
wine, tomatoes and about 150 ml/²/₃ cup cold water.
Bring to the boil then stir in the drained beans and
bring back up to simmering point. Season with salt
and pepper.

Put a lid on the casserole and bake the beans in the
preheated oven for about an hour until the sauce
is rich and thick but the beans are still holding their
shape, checking half way through that they are not
getting too dry. Add extra water if needed.

Check the seasoning (I like to add a small extra dash
of wine at this point) then stir in the parsley and
mint. Cool slightly and serve topped with crumbled
feta with some pitta or other flatbread on the side.

What to drink

A Greek red such as Agioritiko would be in
keeping or any kind of rustic Mediterranean red.

Steamed asparagus with sauvignon, lemon and dill sauce

This really easy yet impressive-looking sauce is a version of the French beurre blanc, which consists of adding butter to a white wine reduction. Since the taste of the butter is crucial, buy the best you can find.

2 small bunches of asparagus, about 500 g/16 oz. in total

3 tablespoons Sauvignon Blanc or other citrus-flavoured white wine

1 shallot, very finely chopped (as finely as possible)

110 g/scant 1 stick very good quality unsalted butter, chilled and cut into small cubes

1 teaspoon freshly squeezed lemon juice

1 tablespoon freshly chopped dill

sea salt and freshly ground white pepper

Serves 4

Rinse the asparagus and trim off the woody end of the stalks. Put them in the basket of an asparagus steamer or a regular steamer and steam for about 5 minutes until the stems are just tender. Remove the steamer from the heat and take off the lid.

Meanwhile, put the wine and finely chopped shallot in a non-reactive (stainless steel) saucepan and cook over a medium to low heat until the liquid has reduced by half. Reduce the heat as low as possible and whisk in the chilled butter a few cubes at a time with a wire whisk. As the butter is incorporated and the sauce thickens, whisk in a few more cubes until it has all been added. Season to taste with a small squeeze of lemon juice and salt and pepper, then stir in the dill.

To serve, put the asparagus spears on warm plates and spoon the warm sauce over the top.

What to drink

You could either stick to Sauvignon Blanc or drink an unwooded or lightly oaked Chardonnay.

Vignarole (spring vegetable stew)

This typically Roman dish is a recipe to make in Spring when the new season's vegetables hit the shops and markets. Even better, use veg you've grown yourself. As a simple dish it relies on the best ingredients so the exact cooking time will vary depending on how fresh they are. (If you're using late season broad/fava beans, blanch and skin them first and add them at the last minute with the herbs.)

freshly squeezed juice of ½ lemon

6–8 baby artichokes

5 tablespoons olive oil plus extra for drizzling over the stew

75 g/½ cup diced pancetta (you can leave this out if you want the dish to be vegetarian)

1 medium sweet white onion, chopped

1 bunch of spring onions/scallions, trimmed, larger ones halved and cut into 2–3 lengths

75 ml/⅓ cup dry white Italian wine

175 ml/¾ cup light vegetable stock

175 g/1 generous cup fresh peas

175 g/1⅓ cups fresh or frozen broad/fava beans

4–5 outer Cos lettuce leaves

2 heaped tablespoons freshly chopped flat leaf parsley

1 heaped tablespoon freshly torn mint leaves

sea salt and freshly ground black pepper

Serves 4

Fill a medium to large bowl with cold water and add the lemon juice to stop the artichokes discolouring. Trim off the stalks and the outer leaves, quarter and cut away the tough tips of the artichoke and remove the hairy choke, popping the quarters into the water as you finish them.

Heat 2 tablespoons of the olive oil and fry the pancetta (if using) until lightly browned. Add 3 more tablespoon of oil, the chopped onion, spring onions/scallions and prepared artichoke hearts, stir, season, cover and cook over a low heat for about 10–15 minutes until they start to soften. Add the white wine and vegetable stock and bring to the boil.

Tip in the fresh peas and broad/fava beans and simmer for another 5–10 minutes until the vegetables have softened but still have some bite. Remove the central stem from the lettuce leaves, then shred and add the leaves to the pan and cook for another 2–3 minutes until they have wilted down. Stir in the parsley and mint and check the seasoning. Drizzle over some extra olive oil before serving.

What to drink

A crisp fresh white wine like a Frascati or a Falanghina.

Caponata

This version of the famous Sicilian dish is similar in ingredients to a ratatouille but crunchier more like a cooked salad.

3 large aubergines/
   eggplants (about
   750–800 g/1³/₄ lb.)
100 ml/¹/₃ cup plus 1
   tablespoon olive oil
1 onion, chopped
2 celery stalks, sliced
2 red (bell) peppers,
   deseeded and sliced
¹/₂ teaspoon ground
   cinnamon
3 tablespoons tomato
   purée/paste
2 tablespoons sugar

75 ml/¹/₃ cup full-bodied red
   wine, preferably Sicilian
2 tablespoons red wine
   vinegar
25 g/2¹/₂ tablespoons capers
110 g/1 cup pitted green
   and black olives
   marinated in herbs
25 g/³/₄ oz. currants
sea salt, freshly ground
   black pepper and chilli/
   hot red pepper flakes,
   to taste

Serves 8

Cut the aubergine/eggplant into cubes and place in a colander. Salt generously and leave for an hour. Heat 3 tablespoons of the olive oil in a large frying pan/skillet or sauté pan, cover and cook the onion and celery until beginning to soften. Add the (bell) peppers, stir, cover and continue to cook for about 5 minutes until they begin to soften too. Add the cinnamon and tomato purée/paste and sugar then add the wine and vinegar and bubble up. Pour in about 150 ml/²/₃ cup of water then add the capers, olives and currants and simmer for about 5 minutes. Meanwhile rinse the aubergines/eggplants and pat them dry. Heat the remaining oil in another pan and fry the aubergines/eggplants until lightly browned on all sides. Tip them into the other vegetables and cook for a further 5 minutes. Check the seasoning adding salt and pepper (or a pinch of chilli/hot red pepper flakes) to taste, then cool. Serve at room temperature.

What to drink

A Nero d'Avola or Primitivo from Sicily would be perfect or a lighter style of Zinfandel.

Braised lentils

This rustic dish is almost a meal in itself but would make a good accompaniment for roast or grilled/broiled pork or sausages.

2 tablespoons olive oil
3 rashers/slices streaky/
   fatty bacon or 75 g/2¹/₂ oz.
   lardons, chopped
1 medium onion, finely
   chopped
1 medium carrot, peeled
   and finely chopped
1 celery stalk, finely
   chopped
2 garlic cloves, crushed
50 ml/3¹/₂ tablespoons dry
   white wine
175 g/1 cup puy lentils

400 ml/1³/₄ cups chicken
   or vegetable stock
¹/₂ teaspoon coarsely
   ground black pepper
a good handful of freshly
   chopped flat leaf parsley
sea salt, to taste

Serves 4–6

Heat the olive oil in a heavy-based pan. Tip in the bacon and fry over a low-moderate heat until beginning to brown. Add the chopped onion, carrot and celery, stir, put a lid on the pan and leave over a low heat for about 10 minutes until the vegetables are beginning to soften. Add the crushed garlic, stir and cook for a couple of minutes then pour in the dry white wine. Bubble up and reduce.

Rinse the lentils and tip into the pan, add the vegetable stock and bring to the boil. Season with pepper and simmer for about 35–40 minutes until the stock has evaporated. Season to taste. Stir the parsley into the lentils and heat through.

What to drink

It partly depends what you serve the lentils with but a young Syrah would work really well.

Chestnut, mushroom and madeira tarts

These delicious little open tarts solve the problem of what to cook on Christmas Day – or for other festive winter occasions – if you're a vegetarian or cooking for veggie friends or family members.

1 sheet of puff pastry
(about 320 g/11 oz.)
1 egg yolk, beaten
1 tablespoon olive oil
50 g/3½ tablespoons
butter
250 g/9 oz. shallots,
peeled and larger ones
halved
400 g/14 oz. chestnut/
cremini mushrooms,
wiped clean and
quartered
75 ml/⅓ cup medium-
dry Madeira or
Amontillado sherry
1 rounded tablespoon
plain/all-purpose flour
300 ml/1¼ cups strong
mushroom or onion
stock made with
a stock pot

125 g/1 cup unsweetened
cooked chestnuts,
halved
125 g/3 cups cavolo nero
1 tablespoon freshly
chopped flat leaf
parsley
sea salt and freshly
ground black pepper,
to taste

Serves 4 or
6 as a starter

Preheat the oven to 200°C (400°F) Gas 6.

Unroll the pastry sheet and place on a lightly floured board. Cut into four (or six) pieces, place on a baking sheet then score each piece about 1.5 cm/5/8 in. from the outer edge. Prick the centre of each piece several times with the prongs of a fork. Glaze the edges with beaten egg yolk then bake for 10 minutes until puffed up. Turn the heat down to 180°C (350°F) Gas 4, cook for another 10 minutes then remove from the oven.

Meanwhile heat the olive oil in a saucepan, add the butter and tip in the shallots. Cook over a medium heat until beginning to brown, then add the mushrooms, season with salt and pepper and stir. Cook uncovered for about 10–15 minutes, stirring occasionally then pour in the Madeira and let it reduce. Stir in the flour then add as much stock as you need to make a thick sauce. Simmer for 5 minutes, check the seasoning and set aside.

Strip the stems off the cavolo nero leaves. Tear roughly into pieces and place in a large pan. Cover with boiling salted water, bring to the boil then cook for a couple of minutes until tender. Drain and refresh with cold water. Fold into the mushrooms along with the chestnuts and reheat.

Place the tart bases back into the oven. Check the seasoning of the mushrooms, adding a little more stock or water if the sauce has thickened too much. Spoon into the pastry bases and serve immediately, sprinkled with a little chopped parsley.

What to drink

A good Côtes du Rhône Villages would be perfect.

Fennel and parmesan sourdough gratin

A delicious side for either meat or fish – it would go particularly well with a rack of lamb, a bacon joint or seared salmon.

2 tablespoons olive oil
25 g/2 tablespoons butter, plus extra for topping
1 large onion (about 225 g/ 8 oz.), sliced
2 large fennel bulbs (about 800–850 g/28–30 oz.) with leaves
3 tablespoons dry white wine
1 level teaspoon ground fennel seeds (optional)
3 tablespoons vegetable or chicken stock
2 tablespoons double/heavy cream
40 g/1 slice slightly stale sourdough bread
40 g/^{1}/$_2$ cup Parmesan
sea salt and freshly ground black pepper

Serves 4–6 as a side

Heat the olive oil in a large frying pan/skillet, add the butter then cook the onion over a low heat. Cut the stalks and leaves off the fennel and trim the rest of the bulb, cutting away the dense core. Slice the bulbs thickly and add to the onion. Cut the leaves and smaller sprigs off the stalks, slice the stalks and add them to the pan along with the ground fennel seeds, if using. Season and fry for 5–8 minutes until the onion and fennel are beginning to soften. Add the wine and stock, stir, cover and cook for 10–15 minutes until the vegetables are tender. Stir in the cream.

Meanwhile tear the bread into small pieces, crumble the Parmesan and chop the remaining sprigs and leaves of fennel. Place in a food processor and blitz until you have rough crumbs.

Heat the grill/broiler. Scatter the topping over the fennel, dot with butter and grill/broil until the top is browned.

What to drink

A creamy white wine such as a Chardonnay or Chenin Blanc. If it's a side, match the wine to the main dish.

Slow-cooked red cabbage with beetroot

Beetroot/beets make the world of difference to red cabbage, adding sweetness and vibrant colour to this warming, wintry side dish.

3 tablespoons light olive oil
2 medium red onions, finely sliced
500 g/18 oz. finely shredded red cabbage (cut away the central tough core)
1 tablespoon dark muscovado sugar
150 g/5^1/$_2$ oz. beetroot/ beets, peeled and cut into strips
150 g/5^1/$_2$ oz. Bramley apples, peeled and chopped
2 finely pared strips of orange zest
4–5 cloves
125 ml/^{1}/$_2$ cup full-bodied fruity red wine such as a Côtes du Rhône
sea salt and freshly ground black pepper

Serves 6

Preheat the oven to 160°C (325°F) Gas 3.

Heat the oil in a large flameproof casserole. Add the sliced onions, stir and cook slowly until beginning to soften. Tip in the red cabbage, stir, cover and cook until it begins to wilt. Stir in the sugar then add the beetroot/beets, apple, orange zest and cloves. Stir, season and add 100 ml/^{1}/$_3$ cup plus 1 tablespoon of the wine. Bring to the boil and transfer to the preheated oven for 2–2^1/$_2$ hours until the cabbage is soft, checking and stirring it occasionally. Add the rest of the red wine if it appears to be drying out.

What to drink

You're more likely to serve this as a side than a meal on its own, but it's a strong-flavoured dish that needs a full-bodied red.

Courgettes and mushrooms a la grècque

This dish offers a modern twist to the classic French way of serving a vegetable salad with a hot wine-based dressing. I like to pour the dressing over the vegetables rather than cook them in it, which makes for brighter colours and a fresher, crunchier texture. Tone down the heat by using fewer chillies/chiles, if you prefer.

300 ml/1¼ cups crisp, dry white wine, such as Pinot Grigio

2 garlic cloves, very finely chopped

2 bay leaves

1 tablespoon coriander seeds

1 teaspoon coarse sea salt, plus extra for seasoning

½ teaspoon black peppercorns

¼–½ teaspoon crushed dried chillies/chiles, to taste

75 ml/5 tablespoons extra virgin olive oil

1–2 tablespoons freshly squeezed lemon juice

250 g/9 oz. small courgettes/zucchini

350 g/12 oz. button mushrooms

2 rounded tablespoons freshly chopped mint leaves

2 rounded tablespoons freshly chopped parsley

freshly ground black pepper

warm pitta bread or other flatbread, to serve

Serves 4

Heat the wine, garlic and bay leaves in a small saucepan and simmer gently until the wine has reduced by half. Remove and discard the bay leaves. Grind the coriander seeds, sea salt, peppercorns and dried chillies/chiles using a pestle and mortar. Add this to the reduced wine, along with the olive oil and 1 tablespoon of lemon juice. Stir and simmer over a very low heat for 4–5 minutes.

Meanwhile, top and tail the courgettes/zucchini and cut them lengthways into very thin slices using a mandoline or a vegetable peeler. Wipe the mushrooms and slice them thickly. Put the courgettes/zucchini and mushrooms in a large, heatproof serving bowl, pour over the hot dressing and sprinkle with the mint leaves. Toss the vegetables in the dressing, then let cool for about 1 hour, tossing them occasionally.

Check the seasoning, adding more salt, pepper and lemon juice, if necessary. Add the parsley, toss well and serve with warm pitta bread or other flatbread.

What to drink

Try a simple, crisp fresh white – the same you use to make the dish would be fine. A dry rosé would also work really well.

Sauces, butters
and relishes

Simple tomato and white wine sauce

This is a simple sauce to make in the summer when tomatoes are ripe and you want a lighter sauce than you get with canned tomatoes. If your tomatoes aren't that ripe add a tablespoon of tomato purée/paste for extra flavour. Use with pasta, prawns/shrimp, white fish or chicken. Add some herbs such as parsley if you have them and a few chopped olives or capers if you want to make it a bit punchier.

250 g/9 oz. ripe tomatoes
2 tablespoons olive oil
1 small garlic clove, crushed
3 tablespoons dry white wine
3 tablespoons light vegetable stock or water
sea salt and freshly ground black pepper

Serves 2

Skin the tomatoes by making a small cut in the skin, popping them in a bowl and covering them with boiling water. Drain the tomatoes after 1 minute, plunge them into cold water, peel and chop roughly, removing any tough, unripe bits near the stalk.

Heat the olive oil in a pan over a moderate heat and fry the garlic for a couple of minutes. Add the wine and bubble up until reduced, then stir in the chopped tomatoes and stock or water. Cover and cook over a low heat for about 10 minutes or until the tomatoes are soft, then mash them into the sauce. Season with salt and pepper and serve.

Burnt onion and chipotle sauce

Red wine plays an important role in this barbecue sauce and, despite the spicy chipotles, the flavour really comes through. A perfect accompaniment for a burger.

3 tablespoons olive oil or other cooking oil
1 large onion (about 225 g/8 oz.), finely chopped
2 garlic cloves, crushed
75 g/4 teaspoons chipotle peppers en adobo
15 g/1 tablespoon dark molasses sugar
1 teaspoon fine sea salt
125 ml/½ cup Malbec or other full-bodied fruity red wine
150 ml/⅔ cup passata/strained tomatoes

sterilized glass jar (see page 4)

Serves 2

Heat the oil in a frying pan/skillet, add the onion, stir and cook over a relatively high heat for about 10–15 minutes until the onions are really well browned. Turn the heat down, add the crushed garlic, stir and cook for a couple of minutes. Meanwhile put the peppers in a food processor or blender. Add the sugar, salt and browned onions and whizz to a thick paste. Add half the wine and the passata/strained tomatoes and whizz again. Tip back into the frying pan/skillet. Pour the remaining wine and 100 ml/about ⅓ cup water into the food processor to pick up the last bits of sauce and add to the pan. Stir, bring to the boil then simmer for 10 minutes. Take off the heat*, cool, transfer to a sterilized jar and store in the fridge. It will keep for a week.

*You can sieve/strain it to get a smoother sauce but I like the rough texture as it shows it's homemade!

Jamon and pink peppercorn butter

I got this idea from one of my favourite local Bristol restaurants, Bell's Diner. They serve it instead of butter with the sourdough bread they offer at the beginning of the meal. It's the perfect use for offcuts from a Spanish ham on the bone. Use slightly more wine and slightly less butter if the ham is fatty.

125 g/1 cup ham offcuts from a Spanish
    ham bone
60 ml/¹/₄ cup dry white wine
1 teaspoon pink peppercorns crushed with
    a mortar and pestle or ¹/₂ teaspoon crushed
    black pepper
125 g/1¹/₈ sticks unsalted butter at room
    temperature, cut into cubes
sourdough or rye bread, to serve

Enough for 6–8

Put the ham in the bowl of a food processor and blitz until it's finely chopped. Add the wine and whizz until it forms a thick paste. Add the crushed peppercorns and work in the softened butter using the pulse button.

What to drink

Fino sherry always goes well with ham but a glass of Albariño or dry rosé would be enjoyable too.

Chorizo butter

A robust, spicy butter you can melt onto a steak or a pork or lamb chop.

70 g/generous ¹/₂ cup chopped chorizo
1 garlic clove, crushed
3 tablespoons red wine
70 g/²/₃ stick soft butter, cut into cubes
2 tablespoons freshly chopped parsley
freshly ground black pepper

Enough for 6–8

Put the chorizo in the bowl of a food processor. Add the crushed garlic and wine and whizz until it forms a thick paste. Add the softened butter using the pulse button. Add the parsley and season generously with black pepper.

Tip the chorizo butter onto a piece of foil and shape into a rectangle. Use the foil to roll the butter into a sausage shape, twist the ends like a Christmas cracker and chill until firm.

Remove from the refrigerator 20–30 minutes before serving. Cut into thin slices and melt onto a steak or a pork chop.

Simple lemon, cream and chive sauce

A deliciously indulgent white wine sauce with which you can anoint a simple piece of fish, jazz up a salmon-en-croute or even use as a pasta sauce for two (it's good with prawns/shrimp).

3 tablespoons dry white wine
40 g/3 tablespoons soft butter, cut into cubes
grated zest of ¹/₂ lemon
75 ml/¹/₃ cup double/heavy cream
1 heaped tablespoon freshly snipped chives
sea salt and white pepper

Serves 2

Measure the white wine into a small saucepan, heat and reduce by half. Whisk in the butter, then add the lemon zest and double/heavy cream and stir. Warm through gently, taking care not to bring the liquid to the boil, then stir in the chives.

If you use this sauce to coat fish you've just poached or microwaved, add a couple of spoonfuls of the cooking juices too.

Cheese and garlic spread

This is barely a recipe, more an ingenious way to use up the tail ends of pieces of cheese. The French call it 'fromage fort'.

250 g/9 oz. assorted bits of cheese, at room temperature
2 garlic cloves, peeled and roughly chopped
³/₄ tablespoon dry white wine
¹/₂ teaspoon coarsely ground black pepper
2 tablespoons freshly chopped parsley

Serves 2

Sort through the cheese, removing the rind and cut into cubes. Put the garlic in a food processor and whizz until finely chopped. Add the cheese and pulse a few times then add the wine and whizz until you have a spreadable consistency. Add the black pepper and parsley and pulse to incorporate. Transfer to a bowl, cover and ideally leave in the fridge for a couple of hours for the flavours to develop. Serve on crackers or crostini.

Light chicken jus

These are two riffs on an accompaniment to roast chicken – the first a lighter, French-style sauce without flour, the second a more classically English gravy. Personally I'd have the former in summer and the latter in winter.

1 oven-ready chicken, approx. 2 kg/4$^{1}/_{2}$ lbs.
75 ml/$^{1}/_{3}$ cup dry white wine
200 ml/scant 1 cup chicken stock
sea salt and freshly ground black pepper
lemon juice (optional)

Serves 4

Preheat the oven to 200°C (400°F) Gas 6.

Season the bird with salt and pepper and place in a roasting pan. Put in the preheated oven for 40 minutes. Remove the bird from the oven, tip the pan and carefully pour off all but a couple of spoonfuls of pan juices. Baste the chicken with the juices and pour the white wine round the chicken and return to the oven for a further 40–50 minutes. Once the chicken is cooked set it aside to rest. Skim off any excess fat from the pan juices. Return the pan to a very low heat and work the stuck-on pan juices off the sides with a wooden spoon, adding a splash more wine if there isn't much left in the pan. Add the stock and bubble up until slightly reduced. Check the seasoning and adjust to taste. Strain through a fine-meshed sieve/strainer, if desired.

Roast chicken gravy

75 ml/$^{1}/_{3}$ cup white or red wine
20 g/2$^{1}/_{3}$ tablespoons plain/all-purpose flour
350 ml/1$^{1}/_{2}$ cups hot chicken or turkey stock, preferably homemade
sea salt and freshly ground black pepper
Amontillado sherry or Madeira (optional)

Serves 4–6

Follow the recipe for Light Chicken Jus up to the point where you skim off the excess fat. Sprinkle the flour into the pan and work into the pan juices. Whisk in the hot stock, bring to the boil and simmer for about 5 minutes, adding a little extra stock if it's too thick. Season with salt and pepper to taste. A dash of Amontillado sherry or Madeira can be good if you want a richer, more full-flavoured stock. If you've roasted garlic with the chicken you can pop a couple of soft cloves out of their skins and mash them into the pan for extra flavour.

Cep gravy

This is one of my favourite ways to make gravy and particularly good with roast beef.

25 g/$^{3}/_{4}$ oz. dried ceps
2 tablespoons olive oil
3 banana shallots, peeled and finely sliced
20 g/1$^{1}/_{2}$ tablespoons butter
1 garlic clove, crushed
1 tablespoon plain/all-purpose flour
75 ml/$^{1}/_{3}$ cup red wine
roasting and/or meat juices
sea salt and freshly ground black pepper

Serves 4

Soak the ceps for at least half an hour in hand hot water to cover. Slice roughly, retaining the soaking liquid. Heat the oil in a shallow pan and add the sliced shallots. Cook over a low heat until beginning to soften. Stir in the butter then add the crushed garlic. Cook for another 5 minutes or so until the shallots start to turn golden. Add the flour, stir and cook for a minute then pour in the wine. Allow to reduce and thicken then add the ceps and their soaking liquid. Bring up to the boil then turn the heat down and simmer for 15 minutes. Once your meat is cooked and rested add any skimmed meat juices or add the gravy to the juices in the roasting pan, adding extra water if needed. Reheat and serve. You can strain the gravy if you want for a smoother texture.

Plum and pinot jam

Wine gives jam/jelly an exotic lift. I originally made this jam with windfall plums, but it was so good I make it every year now.

1 kg/2¼ lb. plums
250 g/1¼ cups preserving sugar
300 g/1½ cups granulated sugar
2 tablespoons pomegranate molasses
6–8 cardamom pods, lightly crushed
1 teaspoon ground cinnamon
50 ml/3½ tablespoons Pinot Noir
50 ml/3½ tablespoons water

sterilized glass jars (see page 4)

Serves 4

Halve the plums, twist and remove the stones/pits, then cut into two or three pieces. Place in a large saucepan or preserving pan with the sugars, pomegranate molasses, cardamom pods, cinnamon and Pinot. Place over a very low heat until the sugars have completely dissolved then bring to the boil and boil hard for about 15 minutes until the jam is set. Remove the cardamom pods, skim the jam and rest for 10 minutes, then put into hot, sterilized jars.

Fig and walnut relish

This is one of those recipes that came about by happy accident while trying to use up the Christmas leftovers. It makes the perfect accompaniment to the remains of the Stilton – or any other crumbly blue cheese.

125 g/scant 1 cup dried figs, preferably organic
50 ml/3½ tablespoons tawny port
30 g/¼ cup walnut kernels

sterilized glass jar (see page 4)

Serves 4

Snip the figs into quarters and place in a sterilized jar. Mix the port with 50 ml/3½ tablespoons of water, pour over the figs, put a lid on the jar and give it a good shake. Leave the figs to marinate for at least 24 hours. Toast the walnut pieces lightly in a dry pan and chop roughly. Cool and stir into the figs.

Apricot and moscatel relish

Wine can be used instead of vinegar to add a sharp counterpoint to the sweetness of a jam or relish. This is delicious with seared or smoked duck, grilled/broiled pork or cold ham.

2 tablespoons light olive oil or sunflower oil
1 medium white onion (about 100 g/3½ oz.), finely chopped
600 g/3⅓ cups fresh apricots, stoned/pitted and halved
25–40 g/2–3¼ tablespoons soft brown sugar
2 strips of orange peel, with as little pith as possible
4–5 cloves
4–5 tablespoons Moscatel such as Moscatel de Valencia
sea salt

sterilized glass jars (see page 4)

Serves 4

Heat the oil in a medium-sized saucepan, add the onion, stir, turn the heat down, cover and cook over a low heat for about 10 minutes until the onion is soft. Tip in the apricots, 25 g/2 tablespoons of sugar, the orange peel, cloves, a pinch of salt and 4 tablespoons Moscatel. Stir and bring to the boil, reduce the heat, cover and cook for about 20–25 minutes until the apricots are soft. Check the seasoning adding a splash more wine or sugar to taste. Remove the cloves and orange rind and transfer to sterilized jars.

Sweet things
and baking

Red wine and cherry ripple ice cream

With so many ice creams available to buy, it might seem unnecessary to make your own, but this version is worth it.

6 large/US extra-large
  egg yolks
125 g/²/₃ cup minus 2
  teaspoons caster/
  granulated sugar
560 ml/2¹/₃ cups single/light
  cream
2 tablespoons whole/full-fat
  milk
1 teaspoon pure vanilla extract

FOR THE CHERRY SAUCE
350 g/1³/₄ cups pitted dark red
  cherries or a large jar of
  Morello cherries, drained
125 g/1 cup fresh or frozen
  raspberries
3–4 tablespoons caster/
  granulated sugar
100 ml/¹/₃ cup plus
  1 tablespoon fruity red wine,
  such as Merlot
1 tablespoon kirsch or cherry
  brandy (optional)

an ice cream maker (optional)

Serves 4–6

What to drink

Wine, even sweet wine, doesn't stand up that well to ice-cream but you could try a modern super-fruity style of ruby port.

To make the cherry sauce, put the cherries, raspberries and 3 tablespoons caster/granulated sugar in a saucepan. Heat gently, stirring occasionally, until the sugar has dissolved. Add 75 ml/¹/₃ cup wine, bring to the boil and simmer for 10–15 minutes until the cherries are soft and the liquid is syrupy. Taste and add extra sugar, if necessary. Let cool, then chill in the refrigerator.

Put the egg yolks and 110 g/¹/₂ cup plus 1 tablespoon caster/granulated sugar in a heatproof bowl and beat with a hand-held electric mixer until smooth, pale and moussey. Put the cream, milk and remaining sugar in a saucepan and heat gently until almost boiling. Pour the hot cream over the egg mixture in a steady stream, whisking constantly until smooth.

Pour the custard through a fine-mesh sieve/strainer back into the rinsed pan. Heat very gently, stirring constantly with a wooden spoon, until the custard thickens and coats the back of the spoon. If it looks like it's starting to boil, remove the pan from the heat and stir for a couple of minutes to let cool slightly before returning it to the burner. Stir in the vanilla extract, then let the custard cool completely. Pour the cold custard into a plastic container and place it in the freezer. Remove it after about 1 hour when the edges have begun to harden. Beat with a hand-held electric mixer. Return to the freezer, then beat again after 30 minutes. (Or churn in an ice cream maker.)

When the mixture is the consistency of soft-scoop ice cream, take half the cherry sauce and cut up any larger pieces of fruit. Fold a few teaspoons of the mixture into the ice cream, turn the ice cream over with a tablespoon and repeat until half of the cherry mixture has been incorporated. Freeze the ice cream for several hours and refrigerate the rest of the sauce.

Transfer the ice cream to the refrigerator for 15–20 minutes to soften slightly before serving. Meanwhile, put the remaining cherry mixture, the remaining wine and a splash of kirsch or cherry brandy, if using, in a saucepan and heat gently until almost boiling. Let cool for 10 minutes. Serve the ice cream in scoops with the warm cherry sauce poured over.

PX Tiramisu

PX stands for Pedro Ximenez – a wickedly treacly style of sherry,
which of course comes from Spain, not Italy but nevertheless makes
a fantastic tiramisu with a lovely raisiny flavour.

250 g/1 generous cup
  mascarpone
100 ml/^{1}/$_3$ cup plus 1
  tablespoon PX sherry
3 large/US extra-large eggs
50 g/^{1}/$_4$ cup unrefined caster/
  granulated sugar
125 ml/^{1}/$_2$ cup strong espresso
  coffee
1 tablespoon brandy
16–18 Savoiardi biscuits/
  cookies
2–3 teaspoons unsweetened
  cocoa powder
a little grated dark/bittersweet
  chocolate, to serve

*a medium-sized rectangular
dish about 24 x 16 x 8 cm/
9^1/$_2$ x 6^1/$_4$ x 3^1/$_4$ in.*

Serves 4–6

Tip the mascarpone into a bowl with 3 tablespoons of the PX sherry
and beat with a wooden spoon until smooth.

Separate the eggs, putting the yolks into a large bowl and two of the
whites into another bowl. Add the sugar and beat at high speed with electric
beaters until the mixture is, pale, light and moussey. Tip half the
mascarpone into the egg mixture and beat it in on medium speed then
repeat with the remaining mascarpone. Wash the beaters and dry
thoroughly then beat the egg whites until stiff and fold into the
mascarpone. Set aside while you prepare the biscuits/cookies.

Pour the coffee into a shallow dish and add the remaining PX and brandy.
Dip half the biscuits/cookies on both sides into the coffee and lay them
in the dish, breaking them in half as necessary to fit. Top with half the
mascarpone mixture and sift over a teaspoon of cocoa powder. Repeat with
the remaining biscuits/cookies and top with the rest of the mascarpone.
Sprinkle with another teaspoon of cocoa, cover the dish with clingfilm/
plastic wrap and refrigerate for at least 6 hours. Remove the clingfilm/plastic
wrap and grate over the dark/bittersweet chocolate before serving.

What to drink

Frankly there's more than enough booze in the
dessert but you could always pour small glasses of PX!

- 225 g/1½ cups sultanas/ golden raisins
- 225 g/1½ cups seedless (dark) raisins
- 350 g/2½ cups currants
- 50 g/⅓ cup undyed glacé/ candied cherries
- 8–10 tablespoons medium-dry Amontillado sherry
- 275 g/2 cups plain/all-purpose flour
- ¼ teaspoon salt
- ½ teaspoon ground cinnamon
- ½ teaspoon ground nutmeg
- 2½ teaspoons unsweetened cocoa powder
- 1 teaspoon gravy browning powder (in the original but optional)
- 225 g/2 sticks unsalted butter at room temperature
- 225 g/1 cup plus 2 tablespoons caster/granulated sugar
- 4 eggs
- 50 g/½ cup chopped almonds
- finely grated zest of ½ unwaxed orange
- 2 tablespoons apricot jam/ jelly, to glaze
- ready-to-eat dried fruits and nuts, to decorate

23-cm/9-in. cake pan, base and sides lined with non-stick baking parchment

Makes 18–20 slices

Super-boozy Christmas fruit cake

I was given this recipe by my late mother in law when I first got married and have used it ever since. It makes the most fabulously moist cake. I prefer to top it with dried fruits rather than the usual royal icing.

Measure out the dried fruits, cherries and nuts into a plastic box or large storage jar and pour over the sherry. Mix well and leave to soak for a couple of days, stirring or shaking the fruit every 12 hours or so.

Sift the flour, salt, cinnamon, nutmeg, cocoa powder and gravy browning, if using, together.

Preheat the oven to 150°C (300°F) Gas 2.

Cream the butter with the sugar until light and fluffy. Beat in the eggs, one at a time, beating well after each addition. Add a spoonful of flour after each egg to prevent curdling. Mix in all the soaked fruit, the almonds, orange zest and the remaining flour mixture and beat thoroughly.

Transfer the cake mixture into the prepared pan. Press down firmly, smooth the top with a spatula or wooden spoon and hollow out at the centre slightly. Bake for 3½ hours until firm to the touch and cooked through. Cover the cake lightly with foil after 2 hours to prevent it over-browning. When the cake it ready remove from the oven and leave in the pan for 20 minutes. Transfer the cake to a wire rack to cool completely. Remove the baking parchment and wrap in fresh greaseproof paper and foil and store in an airtight container for about a month before decorating or icing.

To decorate, briefly microwave 2 tablespoons of apricot jam/jelly and 1 tablespoon water. Sieve/strain and keep warm in a bowl over a pan of simmering water. Brush over the top of the cake. Arrange the dried fruits and nuts over the top of the cake and brush with the remaining glaze.

What to drink

This recipe already has a fair amount of booze in it but if you're feeling especially indulgent, a small glass of sweet sherry or Madeira would be the icing on the cake!

Orange syllabub with crunchy orange sprinkle

Syllabub – a velvety-smooth concoction of sweet wine and cream – is one of the great English puddings, dating from the 16th century. I like it, for a change, made with orange rather than lemon and topped with what my daughter calls 'orange sprinkle', an irresistibly crunchy mixture of orange zest and sugar.

150 ml/²/₃ cup southern French Muscat or other strong sweet white wine (15 per cent ABV)

1 tablespoon Cointreau or other orange liqueur

finely grated zest of 2 unwaxed oranges

4 tablespoons caster/granulated sugar

2 tablespoons freshly squeezed orange juice

2 tablespoons freshly squeezed lemon juice

400 ml/1³/₄ cups double/heavy cream, chilled

1 large bowl, chilled for 30–40 minutes in the refrigerator

6 glass dishes

Serves 6

Pour the wine into a bowl, add the Cointreau or orange liqueur, half the grated orange zest, the orange and lemon juice and 2 tablespoons sugar. Stir, cover and refrigerate for several hours or overnight.

Mix the remaining orange zest and sugar in a bowl. Spread it over a plate and leave for a couple of hours to crisp up. Store it in an airtight container until ready to use.

Strain the wine mixture through a fine, non-metallic sieve/strainer. Pour the cream into the large chilled bowl and beat with a hand-held electric mixer until it starts to thicken. Gradually add the orange-flavoured wine, beating well after each addition until the cream thickens again – you want a thick pouring consistency. When the final addition of wine has been incorporated the mixture should hold a trail when you lift out the beaters, but it shouldn't be stiff. (Don't overbeat it, or it will separate.) Ladle the mixture into six individual glass dishes and chill them in the refrigerator for at least 1 hour before serving.

Just before serving, sprinkle the orange sugar over the top of each dish.

What to drink

I don't think you need to serve wine with this syllabub, but a small glass of well-chilled Sauternes or late-harvested or botrytized Sauvignon or Sémillon would go well.

Roasted pears with sweet wine, honey and pine nuts

Roasting pears in wine transforms them from everyday fruit into a light but luxurious dinner party dessert. Their gentle flavour makes a perfect foil for a fine dessert wine. The trick is to use an inexpensive wine for cooking and a better wine of the same type to serve with it.

freshly squeezed juice
    of 1 large lemon
9 medium just-ripe
    Conference pears
50 g/3½ tablespoons butter,
    softened
3 tablespoons clear fragrant
    honey, such as orange
    blossom
175 ml/¾ cup Premières
    Côtes de Bordeaux or a late
    harvested Sauvignon
    or Sémillon
50 g/½ cup pine nuts
2 teaspoons caster/granulated
    sugar
200 ml/1 scant cup double/
    heavy cream
2 teaspoons vanilla sugar

*a large ovenproof dish, buttered
(large enough to take the
pears in a single layer)*

Serves 6

Preheat the oven to 190°C (375°F) Gas 5.

Strain the lemon juice into a small bowl. Cut the pears in half, peel them and remove the cores. Dip the pear halves in the lemon juice (this will prevent them discolouring), then put them, cut-sides upwards, in the prepared ovenproof dish. Make sure the pears fit snugly in one layer. Put a small knob of butter in the hollow of each pear, then drizzle them with the honey, wine and any remaining lemon juice.

Bake the pears in the preheated oven for 50–60 minutes, turning the pears over halfway through. If you notice while the pears are cooking that they are producing a lot of juice, increase the oven temperature to 200°C (400°F) Gas 6 to concentrate the juices and form a syrup. Remove the pears from the oven and let cool for about 20 minutes.

Meanwhile, lightly toast the pine nuts in a dry, non-stick frying pan/skillet, shaking the pan occasionally, until they start to brown. Sprinkle over the sugar and continue to cook until the sugar melts and caramelizes. Put the cream and vanilla sugar in a small saucepan and heat gently, stirring occasionally, until lukewarm.

To serve, put three pear halves on each plate and spoon over some of their cooking syrup. Trickle over 1 tablespoon warm cream and scatter over a few caramelized pine nuts. Alternatively, serve the cream separately for your guests to pour over.

What to drink

This is a good dessert to pair with a Sauternes or another sweet Bordeaux.

Chocolate and cabernet pots

Combining chocolate with a strong red wine like Cabernet Sauvignon might sound an unlikely idea, but if you think about the wine's red berry flavours it makes sense. It also adds an intriguing edge to this dessert that I bet none of your guests will be able to identify. The ideal Cabernet to use is one that is ripe and fruity but not too oaky.

175 ml/³/4 cup fruity Cabernet Sauvignon, preferably from California, Chile or Australia

40 g/3¹/4 tablespoons caster/granulated sugar

200 g/7 oz. dark/bittersweet chocolate (70 per cent cocoa solids)

280 ml/1¹/3 cups single/light cream

1 egg

a pinch of ground cinnamon

2 teaspoons unsweetened cocoa powder, sifted, to serve

6 or 8 small pots, ramekins or espresso coffee cups, 100 ml/4 oz. each

Serves 6–8

Put the wine and caster/granulated sugar in a saucepan and heat gently until the sugar has dissolved. Increase the heat very slightly and simmer gently for about 20–25 minutes until the wine has reduced by two-thirds to about 4 tablespoons.

Meanwhile, break the chocolate into squares, and put them in a blender. Blitz briefly to break them into small pieces.

Put the cream in a saucepan and heat until almost boiling. Pour the hot cream over the chocolate in the blender, then add the hot, sweetened wine. Leave for a few seconds so the chocolate melts. Whizz briefly until the mixture is smooth. Add the egg and cinnamon and whizz again briefly to mix.

Pour the mixture into 6 or 8 small pots, ramekins or espresso cups, then chill in the refrigerator for 3–4 hours. Remove the chocolate pots from the refrigerator 20 minutes before serving.

To serve, sprinkle a thin layer of cocoa powder over the top of each pot.

Note: This pudding contains raw egg, see note on page 4.

What to drink

A small glass of vintage character or late-bottled vintage port or a sweet red dessert wine would work well with these chocolate pots.

Peaches in prosecco

If you were going to serve fresh fruit in wine, you would think that it would need to be a sweet wine, but try combining a sparkling wine like Prosecco with a fruit liqueur. The secret ingredient in this recipe is the peach schnapps, which subtly enhances the peach flavour.

4 large ripe white peaches

1 tablespoon freshly squeezed lemon juice

200 ml/1 scant cup peach schnapps or peach-flavoured liqueur

1 bottle Prosecco, 750 ml/ 3 cups, chilled

125 g/1 cup raspberries

single/light cream, to serve (optional)

6 individual glass dishes

Serves 6

Halve the peaches by cutting vertically around the fruit with a sharp knife, then twisting the two halves in opposite directions. Cut each half into two pieces and peel off the skin. Cut each piece into three slices and transfer to a deep bowl. Sprinkle over the lemon juice and mix gently (this will stop them discolouring). Pour over the peach schnapps or peach-flavoured liqueur and about two-thirds of the chilled Prosecco. Cover the bowl with clingfilm/plastic wrap and chill in the refrigerator for about 1 hour to let the flavours amalgamate. Keep the remaining Prosecco in the refrigerator.

Before serving, taste for sweetness and add an extra splash of peach schnapps, if necessary.

To serve, spoon the peach slices into six individual glass dishes layering a few raspberries in between. Ladle the peach schnapps and Prosecco over the fruit, then top up with more Prosecco to cover the fruit, if necessary. I prefer to serve this on its own, but you could offer some single/light cream, if you like.

Frosé with strawberries

*No wonder Frosé – basically frozen rosé – took the
internet by storm recently. It's the simplest, most
delicious frozen cocktail.*

**225 ml/1 cup frozen medium dry rosé
(I used a Californian Grenache rosé) – freeze
5–6 hours ahead**
**110 g/1 cup chilled ripe strawberries, plus
a couple for decoration**
**2 tablespoons caster/granulated sugar (you may
need more if you use a drier rosé)**
You will also need 2 chilled or frozen glasses

Serves 2

De-stalk and slice the strawberries, sprinkle with the
sugar, mix well and leave in the fridge for 10–15 minutes.

Stir again and tip into a blender or food processor.

Add the frozen rosé and whizz until you have a deep pink
slush. Pour the frosé into two chilled or frozen glasses,
decorate each with a halved strawberry and serve with
a spoon or a straw.

Strawberry and orange moscato jellies

*A pretty jelly to rustle up for a summer supper.
The amount of sugar you need will depend on
your own personal taste.*

**1/3 of a pack of gelatine (5 sheets,
about 8 g/ 1/4–1/3 oz.)**
450 ml/2 cups sparkling pink Moscato
**2 tablespoons Cointreau or other clear orange
liqueur**
**400 g/scant 4 cups ripe strawberries, plus a few
extra for decoration**
2 tablespoons caster/granulated sugar

Serves 4–6

Soak the gelatine in a bowl of cold water. Heat the
Moscato until hot but not boiling. Add the soaked gelatine
leaves and stir until dissolved. Add the Cointreau or
orange liqueur and set aside to cool. Slice each strawberry
into 3–4 thick slices, remove the stalks, place in a bowl and
sprinkle with the sugar. Turn the strawberries over in the
sugar taking care not to break them up. Once the sugar
has dissolved place half the strawberries in the bottom
of four small glass dishes and pour over half the liquid
jelly/jello to just cover the fruit. Refrigerate for about an
hour until lightly set. Then repeat with the remaining fruit
and jelly/jello (if the jelly/jello has set, warm it slightly then
cool it down before you add it to the glasses). Replace in
the fridge and chill until firm. Decorate with sliced fresh
strawberries, sweetened with a little sugar. You could serve
cream on the side.

Red wine and chocolate-frosted cake

*It might seem odd adding red wine to a chocolate cake but it adds
a really appealing deep fruitiness to both the cake and the icing.*

125 ml/½ cup plus 1 teaspoon
full-bodied fruity red wine,
such as a Chilean Merlot
225 g/1 cup plus 1 tablespoon
unrefined caster/granulated
sugar
15 g/1¾ tablespoons
unsweetened cocoa powder
225 g/2 sticks butter, cubed,
at room temperature
4 eggs, lightly beaten
225 g/1¾ cups self-raising/
rising flour

FOR THE FROSTING
90 g/3 oz. milk chocolate
40 g/3 tablespoons butter
2 tablespoons red wine syrup
(see above)
125 g/1 cup plus 1 tablespoon
icing/confectioners' sugar,
sifted

*a shallow (4 cm/1.5 in.)
18 x 28-cm/7 x 11-in. cake pan
greased and lined with
non-stick baking parchment*

Makes 18 squares

Preheat the oven to 180°C (350°F) Gas 4.

Heat the red wine and 25 g/2 tablespoons of the sugar in a small saucepan over a low heat until the sugar has dissolved. Bring up to the boil and simmer until reduced by half. Take off the heat.

Sift the cocoa powder into a large bowl, pour over 2 tablespoons of the reduced wine and stir to make a paste. Add the remaining caster/granulated sugar, stir then tip in the softened butter, eggs and half the self-raising/rising flour and beat thoroughly with a wooden spoon or electric hand-held whisk. Fold in the remaining flour. Spoon the mixture into the pan and level the surface. Bake for about 30–35 minutes or until well risen and firm to the touch. Leave in the pan for 10 minutes then carefully tip out onto a wire rack to cool.

To make the frosting break up the chocolate and put it in a basin with the butter and 2 tablespoons of the red wine reduction. Place the bowl over a pan of hot water making sure it doesn't touch the water. Once the ingredients have melted remove from the heat and beat in the sifted icing/confectioners' sugar. Swirl the icing over the surface of the cooled cake and leave to set for a couple of hours. Cut the cake into 18 squares.

What to drink

Even though this contains wine it's more about the chocolate so choose a wine that works with chocolate such as a Maury. (But a cup of coffee would be equally good!)

Spiced plum, red wine and amaretti crumble

150 ml/scant ⅔ cup full-
  bodied but unoaked red
  wine
75 g/⅓ cup plus 2
  tablespoons granulated
  sugar mixed with ¾
  teaspoon ground cinnamon
800 g/1¾ lbs. red plums,
  stoned/pitted and halved
  or quartered

FOR THE CRUMBLE
60 g/3 oz. hard amaretti
  cookies
150 g/1 cup plus 2 tablespoons
  plain/all-purpose flour
75 g/⅓ cup plus 2 tablespoons
  caster/granulated sugar
110 g/1 stick chilled butter,
  cubed
chilled thick double/heavy
  cream, to serve

6 individual ovenproof dishes

Serves 6

*Adding wine to this plum crumble really increases the intensity
of its plum flavour.*

Pour the wine into a medium to large saucepan, add the sugar and
cinnamon and warm over a low heat until the sugar has dissolved. Bring
to the boil and simmer until the liquid is reduced by just over half and
is thick and syrupy. (Watch it doesn't catch and burn.) Tip in the plums, stir,
put a lid on the pan and cook for about 7–8 minutes until beginning
to soften. Divide the plum mixture between six lightly greased ovenproof
dishes and leave to cool.

Preheat the oven to 190°C (375°F) Gas 5.

Blitz the amaretti biscuits in a food processor then add the flour, sugar
and cubed butter and pulse until the mixture is the texture of coarse
crumbs. Top the dishes with the crumble mixture and bake in the preheated
oven for 20–25 minutes until the topping is crisp and the plum juices
bubbling through. Serve with thick cream.

What to drink

Already quite rich but a glass of sweet red such
as Recioto della Valpolicella or a late harvest
Zinfandel would work nicely.

Red wine onion, blue cheese and pecan muffins

I must confess I love a savoury muffin. These would be great at lunchtime with a bowl of soup or even just with a salad.

100 g/³/4 cup plus
  2 tablespoons pecans
1 tablespoon oil
125 g/1 stick plus
  2 tablespoons butter
500 g/3 cups finely sliced
red onions
2 tablespoons sugar
3 tablespoons full-bodied red
  wine
300 g/2¹/4 cups plain/
  all-purpose flour
1 tablespoon baking powder
¹/2 teaspoon salt
2 heaped tablespoons natural
  unsweetened yogurt
125 ml/¹/2 cup whole/full-fat
  milk
3 eggs, lightly beaten
50 g/¹/2 cup freshly grated
  mature Parmesan
150 g/1¹/3 cup blue cheese
  such as Stilton or Bleu
  d'Auvergne, roughly
  crumbled

*a non-stick muffin pan with
12 deep holes or a regular
muffin pan lined with
non-stick paper cases*

Makes 12 large muffins

Cook the pecans in a dry frying pan/skillet over a moderate heat for 5–6 minutes, shaking occasionally until lightly toasted. Set aside, cool and chop.

Heat the oil in a large saucepan, add 25 g/2 tablespoons of the butter then tip in the onions and stir thoroughly. Cook, part-covered over a low heat for about 30–40 minutes until completely soft. Add the sugar, cook for a couple of minutes then add the red wine and cook until almost evaporated. Set aside to cool.

In the meantime gently melt the remaining butter in a small pan over a low heat.

Preheat the oven to 190°C (375°F) Gas 5.

Sift the flour, baking powder and salt into a large bowl and make a well in the centre. Put the yogurt in a measuring jug/pitcher and mix in enough milk to make up 225 ml/1 cup.

Pour the melted butter, eggs and yogurt and milk mixture into the flour along with the Parmesan. Mix lightly with a large metal spoon. Fold in the onions, and most of the chopped pecans and blue cheese. Spoon the batter into the muffin pan and sprinkle with the remaining blue cheese and nuts. Bake in the preheated oven for about 25–30 minutes or until fully risen and well browned. Leave in the pan for 5 minutes then transfer to a wire rack for at least another 10–15 minutes to cool.

What to drink

Depends what you eat them with, but on their own they're delicious with a glass of fruity Pinot Noir.

Index

Acknowledgments

Many thanks to everyone who was involved with the book from the my top team at
Ryland, Peters & Small to the long-suffering friends who road tested the recipes.
To Cindy for persuading me to do another book, Julia for helping me shape it. Miriam
for editing it so sympathetically, Mowie Kay for the stunning photography and Leslie
and Sonya for making it all look so beautiful. I truly couldn't have done it without you.